NCTE's Theory and Research into Practice (TRIP) series presents volumes of works designed to offer a teacher audience a solid theoretical foundation in a given subject area within English language arts, exposure to the pertinent research in that area, and a number of practice-oriented models designed to stimulate theory-based application in the reader's own classroom.

Volumes in the Series

Genre Theory

Teaching, Writing, and Being

Deborah Dean
Brigham Young University

National Council of Teachers of English
1111 W. Kenyon Road, Urbana, Illinois 61801-1096

Staff Editor: Becky Standard

Interior Design: Doug Burnett

Cover Design: Pat Mayer

NCTE Stock Number: 18412

It is the policy of NCTE in its journals and other publications to provide a forum for the open discussion of ideas concerning the content and the teaching of English and the language arts. Publicity accorded to any particular point of view does not imply endorsement by the Executive Committee, the Board of Directors, or the membership at large, except in announcements of policy, where such endorsement is clearly specified.

Every effort has been made to provide current URLs and e-mail addresses, but because of the rapidly changing nature of the Web, some sites and addresses may no longer be accessible.

Library of Congress Cataloging-in-Publication Data

Dean, Deborah, 1952–
 Genre theory : teaching, writing, and being / Deborah Dean.
     p. cm. — (Theory & research into practice (TRIP))
 Includes bibliographical references.
 ISBN 978-0-8141-1841-2 ((pbk.))
 1. English language—Composition and exercises—Study and teaching (Secondary)
2. Literary form—Study and teaching (Secondary) 3. Report writing—Study and
teaching (Secondary) I. Title.
 LB1631.D294 2008
 808'.0420712—dc22

                                                                      2007050447

Contents

Acknowledgments

First, and always, a thank you to my students. Because they mattered, I felt the need to learn better ways to teach writing—and found my way to the subject of this book. Thanks to friends whose support over the years has made a big difference: especially Don Newton, who helped me gain the confidence to be in a place where I could write this book, and Leslie Perry, who has kept me on track, helping me take care of real-life stuff when I didn't think I had enough time. I owe gratitude to Brigham Young University for the time I was given to start this project and to Kurt Austin for seeing possibilities in a proposal and preliminary draft. Reviewers' comments and suggestions helped me see ways to improve the manuscript—I appreciate them all very much. Special thanks to Penny Bird, who didn't give up even after repeated drafts didn't quite do the job; her questions were invaluable in helping me see how to reshape my approach. And, as always, to David.

I Theory

One never writes or speaks in a void.
Amy Devitt, *Writing Genres*

1 Why Study Genre Theory?

A friend asked me, "Why is genre theory worth exploring?" Good question. I think it's because genre theory can address many of the problems and challenges we encounter when we teach writing to secondary students. Genre theory is based on the idea that writing is social and that it responds to situations; consequently, writing isn't the same for every person or every situation. Genre theory is "messy" and "complex," to use Amy Devitt's words, and that makes it hard to define—but, for me, it provides answers that help me improve my instruction and student writing (*Writing* 219). Those answers make it worth the mess and complexity.

So what *are* the benefits of using genre theory in the classroom? To begin with, genre theory addresses some aspects of the writing process that get left out of many classrooms. The writing process approach is intended to help students imitate the procedures of more experienced writers and, thus, improve their writing products. Unfortunately, it doesn't always do that. Over twenty years ago, Arthur N. Applebee anticipated a potential problem when he observed that "in many excellent classrooms the various process activities have been divorced from the purposes they were meant to serve. In the original studies of individual writers, the multitude of specific techniques that writers used to aid their planning, revising, or editing were strategies or routines that they orchestrated to solve particular problems. The choice of appropriate strategies was driven by the task at hand—not by a generalized concept of the 'writing process' that the writers used in all contexts" (102). Sometimes those parts of the process originally attached to specific situations and purposes are taught or perceived as routine steps performed for all writing situations.

In contrast to this "generalized" process we sometimes see implemented in classrooms, Mary Jo Reiff describes her process as she wrote her pedagogical response to the preceding theory chapters of the edited collection *Relations, Locations, Positions: Composition Theory for Writing Teachers*. Among other things, she compared the genre she was asked to write to ones she knew and then found similarities; she asked questions about her role and the actions her chapter was intended to perform; she "looked for clues about how the assignment located [her] within a situation and provided [her] with the rhetorical means for acting within that situation"; and she located herself in the larger context of the culture ("Moving" 157). In essence, she modeled procedures successful writers follow whenever they are asked or need to act through writing: they adapt the writing process for the specific purposes at hand—and these include consideration of the social aspects of writing. Genre theory fattens the idea of the writing process, fills it out from its sometimes lean appearance in secondary classes. A more complete idea of process—including the introduction of social considerations—can lead to student success with writing.

An understanding of genre theory is particularly helpful to writers during invention and revision because knowing about genres helps us position ourselves and consider readers' expectations. When I want to write a letter to my friend, I know immediately that I won't have to explain everything I say or even use complete sentences. I won't worry about revision—I probably won't even reread what I write. In contrast, when I wrote a letter of complaint to a large company, I thought for a long time about my position as a customer and the number of people who might read my letter before it got into the hands of someone who could provide the satisfaction I wanted. I selected appropriate details from my experience, and I was conscious of the tone I was using since I wanted to be taken seriously. I had several people read drafts of the letter and give me suggestions for revision before I finally mailed it. Knowing the genre of complaint letters helped me know where to start my writing and which considerations to think about when I revised. Knowing genres gives all writers a "metarhetorical awareness" (Horning 261) that allows them to make effective choices all through the writing process.

The fuller understanding of writing processes that comes from genre theory also leads to a better solution for the product/process dichotomy evident in some classrooms. When it is clearly connected to the situation, students don't see process as a series of products teachers ask them to complete *in addition to* the paper they were originally assigned. They don't see the freewrite or revision as an extra—and they shouldn't be inclined to scribble on a copy of the final draft just to make it look as though it had been revised. When each product is obviously a part of the process, the challenges of getting students to work through that process diminish. The connections between what writers do to create texts and the success of those texts in accomplishing their purposes in specific situations show the value of the choices made during the writing process. Genre theory links process and product in key ways.

Genre theory also challenges students' assumptions that good writing is always the same, that situation, purpose, audience, and relationships don't have an impact on successful writing. Sometimes students think either that teachers are keeping the secret of good writing to themselves or that some teachers (the ones that give them high grades for writing) are the only ones who recognize good writing. Genre theory encourages "the idea that *good* writers adapt well from one genred site of action to the next" (Bawarshi, *Genre* 156; emphasis added). Good writing depends on context—and good writers are ones who know that. Charles Bazerman points out that thinking about genres—of the situations associated with them and the actions carried out by them—can help students "understand when seemingly well-written texts go wrong, when those texts don't do what they need to do" ("Speech Acts" 311). When students think there is only one "right" way to write, genre theory can help them understand the need to adapt writing to situations and the problems that might result if they choose not to adapt.

Genre knowledge also makes important connections for students between reading and writing. Sunny Hyon says that genre "is the first element shaping readers' interpretations of a text, guiding their expectations about the text's topics and the author's comment on that topic" (123). Thus, when young students see the cover of the book *Diary of a Worm* (Cronin), with its picture of a worm in a red ball cap and wielding a pencil as he sits on a bottle cap (if they know picture books at all), they position themselves accordingly: they suspend disbelief, expecting a worm to be personified, to tell of his days, and to show personality. They don't expect a scientific book dense with facts about worms. In a reverse example, when my university students were assigned an article about genre theory, they had a lot of difficulty with it initially. They didn't know how to position themselves as readers since they didn't know the conversation the article was a part of. It was my job to orient them to the academic situation that the article responded to. Because genre connects reading and writing, J. L. Lemke claims that "genre is potentially the great unifying theme of the language arts curriculum. . . . It enables us to teach students about the expectations of readers, and the strategies of writers" (4). In fact, Richard M. Coe asserts that genre "epitomizes" the important ways teachers can connect reading and writing in the classroom because both are social processes and participate in social actions ("Teaching" 159). Genre theory, then, can help students succeed as both readers and writers.

Testing is another classroom concern that genre theory can address. When teachers feel that pressure to succeed on high-stakes standardized tests is encouraging a limited view of writing among their students, genre theory can bring back an appropriate perspective. If, as Carolyn R. Miller claims, "genres serve as keys to understanding how to participate in the actions of a community" ("Genre" 165), then they are also keys to understanding testing situations and how they differ from other writing actions. Coe claims that "understanding genre will help students become versatile writers, able to adapt to the wide variety of types of writing tasks they are likely to encounter in their lives" ("New Rhetoric" 200). That adaptability means that they will be better able to separate the writing expectations of a standardized test from those of, for example, a college entrance essay. Since students sometimes get the impression that "passing the test" *must* mean that they are "good" writers, a genre approach is invaluable. It can help teachers clarify for students that the kind of writing valued on tests represents a limited perspective of what counts as effective writing.

The pressure of testing can also limit teachers' view of writing instruction. Teachers can't ignore students' need to write for such situations, but David Russell provides an effective analogy to remind teachers that genre theory also addresses this test-preparation situation. He explains that some people may be skilled at ball handling in one game (table tennis, for instance) but awkward with the same-sized ball in another game (jacks, for instance). Russell concludes that "there is no autonomous, generalizable skill called ball using or ball handling that can be learned and then applied to all ball games" (57). When he asks, "How can one teach ball-using skills unless one also teaches students the games, because the skills have their motive and meaning only in terms of a particular game or games that use them?"(58), teachers should hear: How can we teach writing as a discrete skill without connecting it to the situation in which it resides? With a genre approach, we can teach students that the values of writing in one situation (testing) are unique to that situation and not necessarily valued in the same way in other writing situations or for other purposes: "One always evaluates the effectiveness of ball using within a particular game, not in general" (59). With that perspective from genre theory, teachers can prepare students to succeed on tests without abandoning good practice. Testing is just one "game" of writing.

Knowing about genres also contributes to critical literacy because it helps students say what they want to say within a situation and understand the implications of doing so. In her book *Writing Genres,* Devitt proposes that the consequences of resisting generic expectations might depend on "the status in the society of the individual who is breaking the convention. . . . Having established membership in a group, a writer then can violate expectations with less severe consequences, though even then the consequences are unpredictable" (86). Once students understand the social aspects of genres, understand that genres carry expectations for acting in certain ways, they can begin to consider the implications of choosing to follow or to resist the expectations associated with those situations. When students resist generic expectations—when their use of informal language in a letter of apology to the principal suggests that they are peers instead of working within a relationship that has an unequal level of authority—there will be consequences. Genre theory helps explain that situation. However, Devitt also notes that "to conform to those expectations also entails consequences, good and bad" ("Genre" 46). Students who know that genres are more than forms, that they represent ways of being and acting in the world, are more capable of choosing resistance or compliance—and the resulting consequences—more effectively.

Currently, teachers are looking for more effective ways to address multimedia writing in their classes. Genre theory provides a sound foundation for such instruction, especially at a time when many teachers are treating different media simply as forms or technological gimmicks with no regard to situation, context, rhetorical strategies, or social action. Kevin Brooks makes a strong case for how genre-based pedagogy can be an important way to approach teaching multimedia projects, Web writing, and hypertexts. Because, he says, students know online genres, their familiarity should serve as "guideposts," "should be at the heart of a genre-based hypertext pedagogy" (342). He suggests "having students understand that all texts, including hypertexts, are rooted in one or more genres" (343). Students who understand genres and their connection to context and situation will be better able to adjust to the challenges of writing in multiple mediums. Also, since "a strong trend in hypertext production seems to be the blurring of genres or the creation of hybrid genres" (343–44), genre theory makes a good foundation for instruction in hypertexts.

These are just some of the reasons genre theory is worth exploring: the ways it enhances the writing process, especially in invention and revision; the ways it connects reading and writing, aiding both readers and writers; the ways it develops writers as critical thinkers and users of language; and the ways it presents fuller approaches to testing and multimodal writing. Nancy Myers states boldly that "without an understanding of genre, students do not succeed" (165). I agree wholeheartedly. So, even though genre theory is somewhat complicated, its benefits to writing and writing instruction—its ability to address many of the concerns and issues of secondary classrooms—make it a valuable addition to pedagogy.

2 Explaining Genre Theory

The uses of genre theory that help it address instructional challenges underscore the new way genre is being defined. More than classifying a "kind" of writing—poetry, a novel, or a letter, for instance— at its heart, genre theory emphasizes the idea that writing is socially constructed. Carolyn R. Miller's landmark 1984 article "Genre as Social Action" is credited with extending the traditional definition of genre in ways that opened new avenues of thought. She argues that genres are "typified rhetorical actions based in recurrent situations" (159). Her emphasis is on the "action [a genre] is used to accomplish" (151) rather than the form a genre takes or even the situation in which it arises.

But that was just the beginning; her idea led to new ways of considering genres. A more thorough explanation is complicated, because, in the end, the theory isn't unified. It's genre theories—plural—and they begin with trying to define genres.

DEFINING GENRES

"Genres pervade lives. People use them, consciously and unconsciously, creatively and formulaically, for social functions and individual purposes, with critical awareness and blind immersion, in the past and yet today. They shape our experiences, and our experiences shape them. As we study and teach these ways of acting symbolically with others, we may be approaching an understanding not just of genres but of the messy, complex ways that human beings get along in their worlds" (Devitt, *Writing* 219).

Perhaps *messy* and *complex* are two perfect words to begin to define genres as current theories conceive of them. Defining *genre* has become very difficult, partly because, as Paul W. Richardson notes, "a perfectly useful word has now been so expanded in meaning as to render it imprecise" (124–25). Anis Bawarshi shows that, even in looking at the etymology, the word is challenging. He notes that *genre* comes from Latin cognates through French, "suggest[ing] that genres *sort* and *generate*" (Devitt, Bawarshi, and Reiff 550). In other words, genres can both arrange what exists and produce something else, something that might not have existed before. The origin of the word reveals a hint of genres' complexity, showing that they are capable of multiple, sometimes seemingly contradictory, actions.

To explain genres, then, it might be simpler to start with what they are not. Many educators still consider genres as "(a) primarily literary, (b) entirely defined by textual regularities in form and content, (c) fixed and immutable, and (d) classifiable into neat and mutually exclusive categories and sub-categories" (Freedman and Medway, "Introduction" 1). Instead, today, genres represent all sorts of interactions (some textual and some not), are defined more by situation than form, are both dynamic and flexible, and are more an explanation of social interaction than a classification system.

Genres Are Not Only about Literary Texts Anymore. In fact, Bazerman indicates that considering genres only from a literary perspective has reduced the recognition of their social aspect: "Because literature is often written and read in contemplative circumstances, apparently (but not thoroughgoingly) removed from immediate exigencies of life, the social embeddedness of genre has been less visible" ("The Life" 20). Thus, although literature also responds to a social context, it is such an abstract one that we often fail to recognize it. Because genres today are more defined by their social situations, genres include all interactions involving texts. In fact, everyday texts, more than literary ones, are often a focus of current genre study.

Genres Are More Than Forms. Although, as Anthony Paré and Graham Smart acknowledge, "repeated patterns in the structure, rhetorical moves, and style of texts are the most readily observable aspects of genre" (147), these observable features do not, by themselves, constitute a genre. Aviva Freedman and Peter Medway explain that regularities in form come from the situation, instead of existing without reason: "Genres have come to be seen as typical ways of engaging rhetorically with recurring situations. The similarities in textual form and substance are seen as deriving from the similarity in the social action undertaken" ("Introduction" 2). Bazerman extends the explanation, showing that forms not only come from situations but also guide us through situations: "Genres are not just forms. Genres are forms of life. . . . Genres are the familiar places we go to create intelligible communicative action with each other and the guideposts we use to explore the unfamiliar" ("Life" 19). And Marilyn L. Chapman affirms the others' assertions about form's relation to genre: "Rather than rules to be followed . . . or models to be imitated . . . , genres are now being thought of as cultural resources on which writers draw in the process of writing for particular purposes and in specific situations" (469). So, although form is an *aspect* of genre, form does not *define* a genre.

Genres Are Not Fixed. Because genres are responses to social situations (and situations are always changing), genres cannot be fixed. At the same time, as noted previously, they are not totally without regularity either. As Devitt explains, "genres, then, are not arbitrary or random, being tied to rhetorical and social purposes and contexts, but neither are they necessary and inevitable, being shaped by various influences at various times" ("Language Standard" 47). Genres are stable, but not unchanging. They may share characteristics over time or in different situations—in fact, a certain amount of stability is essential for genres to carry out action—but they are never exactly the same because no two situations are exactly the same.

Genres Are Not Sortable into Precise Categories nor Are They Classification Systems. Humans can't help but see similarities between responses to situations—special occasions may warrant a greeting card, for instance. But selecting an appropriate greeting card depends partly on the situation—birthday, graduation, death, Mother's Day—so they can't be all the same genre. Even for the same occasion—Mother's Day, for example—a variety of possible responses (cards) is available: sweet, sappy, sentimental, humorous, and so on, depending on the individuals' relationship, and cards can be for birth mothers, adoptive mothers, mothers-in-law, and grandmothers. Because of this connection to situation, Devitt asserts that although classification is an "essential part of understanding genre . . . such classification is defined rhetorically, rather than critically, by the people who use it" (*Writing* 9). Charles Bazerman and Paul Prior agree: classification is more a matter of people attempting to locate and generate genres than of people assigning genres to categories ("Participating" 143). In this way, rhetorically and socially, genres have aspects that allow classification, but not in the traditional sense of being a label for a category by which texts can be identified.

So, if genres are not forms, not fixed, not only about literary texts, and not classification systems, what are they? Gunther Kress defines them by their process of development: "In any society there are regularly recurring situations in which a number of people interact to perform or carry out certain tasks. Where these are accompanied by language of whatever kind, the regularity of the situation will give rise to regularities in the texts which are produced in that situation" ("Genre as Social" 27). So they are texts developed in and responding to recurring situations. That's at the center of genre theory. But theorists are continuing to enlarge the concept. As Bawarshi maintains, "we oversimplify genres when we define them *only* as the typified rhetorical ways in which individuals function within socially defined and a priori recurrent situations" ("Genre

Function" 356; emphasis added). Paré and Smart separate out the functions Bawarshi mentions and describe genre as having "a distinctive profile of regularities across four dimensions" (146). These dimensions include (1) the texts themselves, (2) the processes used to compose the texts, (3) the practices readers use to understand the texts, and (4) "the social roles" the texts and practices establish (146). This expansion of the idea of genre beyond text and into actions, processes, and relationships brings us back to genres as *messy* and *complex*. It is difficult to *define* genres precisely; from a synthesis of theorists' perspectives, we can, however, *characterize* genres as

- social
- rhetorical
- dynamic
- historical
- cultural
- situated
- ideological

I will discuss each aspect of genre separately, but it will soon be clear that these aspects of genre are not discrete. They depend on each other and interrelate in complex ways.

Social

Genres are social. They are used to act in specific situations, and they arise from social interactions. Because of those characteristics, they both reflect the social interaction and help people make sense of shared social experiences. As Bawarshi points out, they "help us define and organize kinds of social actions" ("Genre Function" 335). We make our way in social situations, and figure them out, partly through the genres associated with those situations. Programs at the opera and memos at the office guide participants in different situations. At the same time, the social situation shapes the genre. In some offices, less formal email messages replace memos, while in others, the email message still reads and looks like a traditional memo. So, genres act in situations, but they are also products of that situation.

Genres also respond to social situations; they interact with them. In fact, Bazerman asserts that "each successful text creates for its readers a social fact," becoming "part of the way that humans give shape to social activity" ("Speech Acts," 311, 317). Because of these shaping aspects, genres act as a kind of etiquette, according to Anne Freadman, showing "how people get on with one another" ("Anyone" in Freedman and Medway 57); they are "a social code of behavior established between the reader and author" according to Bawarshi ("Genre Function" 343). Freadman suggests we consider the "rules" of genres to be manners more than laws; by doing so, we can see how genres not only act for purposes but also create options for our actions, options we can choose to adopt or reject, with corresponding social consequences. If we choose to submit a poem when a résumé is expected, we might not get the position—that is, of course, unless the position is for a poet. So genres are social in how they function and in how they respond, in their effects and in their origins.

Because genres are social, part of the meaning they carry resides in the social context that creates the genre. As Bazerman and Prior assert, "only part of the meaning resides in the particular qualities of the texts, while much sits within the sociohistorical genesis of the social, institutional, and material systems within which the texts, users, and interactions are bound together" ("Participating" 137). For example, they list multiple purposes for filling out a form: to "make application, comply with a regulation, or report an event" (144). The texts (forms) may seem similar, but the meaning each carries differs depending on the social situation in which it occurs. And, as people use a genre in a particular activity, they begin to see it as part of that activity, as part of the social web of the community.

Genres are not only ways users act socially. They also have a social aspect in themselves: they interact with each other, both explicitly and implicitly, in noticeable forms and in less noticeable uses of language (Bazerman, "Intertextuality" 86–87). These interactions are referred to as intertextuality, and they occur in a number of ways. Some genres develop out of others, carrying elements of those previous genres into new situations; some respond to ideas and language in other genres, using that language or those ideas as support or as the basis for argument. One specific type of intertextuality, called "genre chains" by Christine M. Tardy and John M. Swales (570), describes genres that always act in response to prior genres. An assignment prompt from a teacher followed by the students' completed assignment followed by the teacher's comments and grade on the assignment—that would be a genre chain.

As a result of this (or interwoven with this) social-activity building aspect, genres position participants, creating social roles for them. David Quammen addresses this role assignment when he writes about compiling his magazine columns for a book: "I mention that sense of relationship because a column is, in my opinion, different from other sorts of magazine writing. Part of a columnist's special task is to turn oneself into an agreeable habit, yet to maintain an edge of surprise and challenge that prevents readers from letting the habit become somnolent rote. . . . The relationship between a magazine writer and the readers tends, in most circumstances, to be fleeting and shallow. In a book, on the other hand, a reader undertakes a sustained and serious connection with the writer. . . . A column can be the most conversational form of journalism, but to create the sense of a conversation with readers, the writer must consent to be a person, not a pundit" (11–12). As Quammen demonstrates, different genres create different relationships. To make any relationship work, the participants agree to take on certain roles. As Paré and Smart explain, "these generic characteristics of role and relationship determine what can and cannot be done and said by particular individuals, as well as when, how, where, and to whom" (149). When I receive an email message from my supervisor, I take a different stance (word choice, level of formality in tone, etc.) in my response than I do when I reply to an email message from a student. Same genre—different roles. The assignment and acceptance of roles and the resulting relationships are part of the social aspect of genres.

Rhetorical

Because they both establish and enforce relationships, genres are rhetorical. That is, they allow users to choose among options to effectively accomplish their purposes in each particular situation. Edward P. J. Corbett and Robert J. Connors identify the "*choice* of available resources to achieve an end" as part of what makes something rhetorical (2). Certainly, if genres are viewed as manners, choice is an element, as is adapting to situation: manners shift for different situations, and people can choose to observe expectations or not. Genre users, then, consider options for communicating their own purposes within the situation, choosing to follow generic expectations or not, to one degree or another.

Devitt posits the presence of both stability and flexibility in the nature of any genre: "stability to ensure that the genre continues to fulfill its necessary functions, flexibility to ensure that individuals can adapt the genre to their particular situations and their changing circumstances" (*Writing* 135). The flexibility she mentions and users' ability to adapt genres show their rhetorical aspects. Terence T. T. Pang describes these rhetorical choices as moves: "Moves are purposeful functional units sustaining the communicative intent of the speaker" (147). Genre users can choose among obligatory moves—those aspects of a genre that are essential to others' identification of it as a genre—and optional moves—those aspects of a genre that are more flexible. For example, in a movie review it would be obligatory to include the reviewer's overall evaluation of the movie, examples to support that evaluation, and references to the acting, cinematography, or other aspects of the production. Optional moves might include choices regarding the arrangement of the review's content (giving the evaluation first or last), the tone the reviewer takes (objective or satiric), or the overall purpose (to inform or persuade). Deciding to follow expected moves and selecting among optional ones are rhetorical choices. The element of strategic choice, of being able to consider situation, purpose, timing, audience, culture, and available options when using a genre, is what makes genres rhetorical.

Dynamic

Partly because they are both social and rhetorical, genres change, and they create change in their contexts. Jeanne Fahnestock provides an interesting example that shows how genres affect context. She lists three different approaches a dean can take to address faculty about budget cuts: listing the cuts in a this-is-how-it-will-be format; explaining the needs and, together with the faculty, brainstorming possibilities for addressing the cuts; or explaining the problem and arguing for a particular course of action (266). Although the initial situation is the same, Fahnestock argues that each rhetorical choice will create a different resulting situation; thus, the choice of genre can change the situation: "The ability of genre to shape context is, then, an important point" (266). This ability of genres to both respond to and affect situation is part of what makes them dynamic.

Another aspect of genres, their ability to be flexible, also contributes to their dynamic nature: because genres can adapt, they also change. Deborah Hicks notes that genres "do not fully *determine* the particular rhetorical moves that can occur in a given setting. Participants can, and do, interpret and subtly alter the discourses that might otherwise be constitutive of a social action" (467). Echoing this sentiment about genres' flexibility, Carol Berkenkotter and Thomas N. Huckin assert this interesting claim: "We feel that genericness is not an all-or-nothing proposition. . . . Instead, communicators engage in (and their texts reveal) various degrees of *generic activity*" ("Rethinking" 492). In other words, some examples of a genre might be more like the expectation than others. Because users adapt genres to their purposes and make rhetorical choices in varying social situations, genres have flexibility—and flexibility can lead, eventually, to change.

Researchers reviewing specific genres through time have documented this dynamic nature. For example, Devitt summarizes JoAnne Yates's review of American business genres from the late nineteenth and early twentieth centuries as an example—noting the factors influencing genre change as well as the ways genres influence cultural transformations (*Writing* 93–96, 102–6, 110–12). In her survey of several such studies, Devitt demonstrates that contextual factors as well as individuals working within genres (resisting them as well as adapting them) contribute to genre change. Devitt, Reiff, and Bawarshi assert that this dynamic aspect of genres is very much a factor of people's use of them: "Genres do not change magically on their own: *people* change genres, usually slowly and imperceptibly, as they begin to recognize the ways in which genres no longer fully serve their needs" (163). Such change can take place at different paces because of varying influences, but there is no doubt that people using genres to accomplish social and personal goals will have an effect on the genres they use.

Historical

Genres are historical in the sense that when they change—or when new genres develop—they depend on previous genres, antecedent genres, for their development. In explaining this characteristic in oral language, M. M. Bakhtin declared, "Any utterance is a link in a very complexly organized chain of other utterances" (69). Echoing Bakhtin, Margaret Himley asserts that "in learning to write (or speak), the learner . . . learns the ways of making meaning of a particular language community by appropriating and reworking those ways to which she has access" (138). Because genres don't exist in a vacuum, because, as Devitt affirms, "our response to [a] situation can be guided by past responses," antecedent genres reveal the historical aspect of genres ("Generalizing" 576). In fact, Devitt argues that "when new genres develop abruptly they may derive more from the context of genres [i.e., previous related ones] than from the context of situation" (*Writing* 99).

Kathleen Jamieson's study of George Washington's first State of the Union address shows the incredible influence of prior genres in developing new ones:

> The umbilical ties were stronger than the framers of the Constitution suspected. Faced with an unprecedented rhetorical situation, Washington responded to the Constitutional enjoinder that the president from time to time report to Congress on the state of the union and recommend necessary and expedient legislation, by

delivering a speech rooted in the monarch's speech from the throne. The Congress, which had rejected as too monarchical the title "His Highness the President of the United States of America and Protector of the Rights of the Same," promptly reacted as Parliament traditionally reacted to the King, and drafted, debated, and delivered an "echoing speech" in reply. (411)

As Devitt concludes, when no genre exists for a new action, the "situation depends heavily on the first rhetor to choose antecedents wisely" (*Writing* 97). Certainly when the first choice isn't as appropriate as it could be, it will be changed—eventually. Until then, though, the consequences of the ineffective genre are at work in the situation. Because genres grow out of past genres and develop into new ones, because they may even depend more deeply on those past genres than we expect, they are historical.

Cultural

In a socially based theory of writing, context matters. Genres are cultural in the sense that they occur in and respond to what Devitt calls a "macro level of context"—a context broader than the immediate situation of the genre—or culture (*Writing* 31). Other theorists refer to this larger concept of context as *discourse community, activity system, community,* or simply *context*. All of these other terms have aspects unique to them but share the idea of broad context, which I generalize here with the label of culture. My generalization, however, isn't intended to simplify the concept of culture. Miller, noting that "Raymond Williams (1976) has called 'culture' one of the two or three 'most complicated' words in the English language," defines it this way: "culture as a 'particular way of life' of a time and place, in all its complexity, experienced by a group that understands itself as an identifiable group" ("Rhetorical" 68). Devitt adds specifics when she defines culture ("loosely") as "a shared set of material contexts and learned behaviors, values, beliefs, and templates" (*Writing* 25). So culture represents the broad context that influences genres—what genres are used, when and how, and by whom.

Despite these clarifications, the concept of culture—discourse community, context, whatever—is, as Berkenkotter and Huckin call it, "slippery" because it isn't a "static entity" ("Rethinking" 497). People move in and out of cultures and belong to several simultaneously. Devitt also acknowledges that people also form groups with commonalities within cultures and between cultures. She delineates three kinds of such groups: *communities*, which are "people who share substantial amounts of time together in common endeavors"; *collectives*, which are "people who gather around a single repeated interest, without the frequency or intensity of contact of a community"; and *social networks,* which are "people who are connected once—or more—removed, through having common contact with another person or organization" (*Writing* 63). These different degrees of interaction among people in various types of relationships exemplify the difficulty in pinning down culture or context.

In addition, genres span communities, enabling relationships between and among them, and genres that develop within a community are sometimes meant for use by those outside it. So the relationships between genres and culture are varied and complex. Miller approaches the complexity in this way: "Rather than seeing [community] as comfortable and homogeneous and unified, I want to characterize it as fundamentally heterogeneous and contentious" ("Rhetorical" 74). Within this disunity, though, she sees genres as a stabilizing aspect: "In their *pragmatic* dimension, genres not only help people in spatio-temporal communities do their work and carry out their purposes; they also help virtual communities, the relationships we carry around in our heads, to reproduce and reconstruct themselves, to continue their stories" (75). So, genres can provide cohesiveness to a culture, but culture also has a role in "defin[ing] what situations and genres are possible or likely" (Devitt, *Writing* 25). Echoing Devitt, Coe indicates that genres define cultures as much as cultures define genres: "part of what defines a discourse community is the genre system it sanctions and empowers" ("New Rhetoric" 199). Indeed, he returns to the reciprocity of culture and genre by pointing out that using a genre "usually means . . . invoking and/or reconstructing both the community's values and its view of the rhetorical situation" (199). Thus, culture influences genres and is, as a result, also influenced by the genres employed by participants in the culture.

Situated

Genres are also *situated* in smaller contexts; that is, they are located in or placed in relation to more particular aspects of their surroundings. Using Devitt's term, the context of situation refers to the "micro level" of context (*Writing* 31). Such a context differs slightly from traditional views of the rhetorical situation (audience, purpose, occasion) by adding social aspects such as participant roles and the relation of the recurring situation to purpose and to uses of language (Devitt, *Writing* 16). To clarify how situation is inherent to genre, Randy Bomer gives an example of seeing a piece of paper under his windshield wiper: it could be either a parking ticket or a flyer advertising something. Depending on the situation, he can anticipate which is most likely. When he's handed a paper by an usher in a Broadway theater, it is probably a program: "Even before we look at it, we have oriented ourselves to ways of reading that genre and will read it only with those questions in mind that are usually answered by a playbill. Every piece of writing, every text we read, comes to us as both a text—the piece it is—and a kind of text—an instance of a genre" (117). Situation positions us to both receive and act with genres—and creates roles and relationships as we do so.

Like culture, situation is also reciprocal, as Devitt explains: "Genre and situation are tightly interwoven . . . but it is genre that determines situation as well as situation that determines genre. To say that genre responds to situation not only is deterministic but also oversimplifies their reciprocal relationship" (*Writing* 23). Devitt illustrates this situatedness when she explains that students writing letters to the editor for a class assignment will perform a different genre than a concerned citizen writing a letter to the editor would (22). The situations—the immediate, and particularly social, aspects of context such as purpose, participant roles, and exigencies, at least—differ, so the genre, as a consequence, does also.

Ideological

Because genres are social, cultural, and situated, it should be no surprise that they are also ideological, that they represent ways of thinking about and valuing the world. Berkenkotter and Huckin note that "genres signal a discourse community's norms" ("Rethinking" 497), and Devitt explains how: "Because people in groups develop genres, genres reflect what the group believes and how it views the world" (*Writing* 59). Since genres are not just forms of social interaction but also ways of being, participating in genres involves assuming the ways of thinking that encompass those ways of being. Bazerman says that acting with genres causes participants to "take on the mood, attitude, and actional possibilities. . . . Adopt a frame of mind, set your hopes, plan accordingly, and begin acting" ("Genre" 13). He likens using genres to going to a place and taking on the character of the place: "If you hang around the race track long enough, you become one of those race track characters" (14).

Since genres are shaped by situation, they represent the values of participants in that situation. When users of genres come from a situation removed from that which created the genre, values may clash. Paré describes Inuit social workers being urged to more closely imitate the record-keeping conventions developed by their urban counterparts. The ideologies of those detached, detailed records represented the values of the urban culture, not the close, almost familial, relationships of the Inuit culture, and this created a conflict for workers: "The workers' dilemma indicates how participation in workplace genres situates writers in relations of power" (63). The use of these genres divided the "individual's sense of identity" (66). In situations like this one with the Inuit workers, James Paul Gee suggests that users may suffer from the "extra cognitive work" that occurs because of conflicts between the ideologies of the genres being used and the personal ideologies of the users (158). These consequences to the ideologies of genres are not all bad, however; sometimes opening new ways of viewing the world might be beneficial. Devitt claims that "ideological power is not necessarily good or evil but rather . . . ambivalent: it works for both good and bad" (*Writing* 158). But these consequences—whether they're perceived to be good or bad—do serve to illustrate that teaching and acting with genres carry social and political implications because of genres' ideological aspects.

Because of ideology, what genres get taught in school and to whom, and whether they are taught as a matter of compliance or resistance, are all matters of concern. Peter Clements asserts that "teachers are never just instructing writers in the means and methods for realizing their thoughts more effectively on paper, but rather are coercing students into specific political choices about how to align themselves within various discourses" (203). Certainly teachers need to be aware of the ideologies of the genres they teach—and avoid what Tom Romano calls "a genre rut" when students become "Johnny-One-Genres" ("Teaching" 174). Journals represent an ideology as much as five-paragraph essays do. Romano urges teachers to "examine our courses and school curricula for genre hegemony. Does one genre dominate?" (174). If it does, what ideologies are we reinforcing for students? What ones are we ignoring?

As a result of these political/ideological aspects, some theorists urge that a critique of genres is essential to students' adequate understanding of them. After explaining that rules control but resources enable, Lemke argues that "to teach genres without critique is not only unethical, it is intellectually faulty. The critique of a genre is what makes it into a resource. It is only when we understand the origins, history, and social functions of a genre, i.e. its politics, that we are empowered to make intelligent, informed decisions in our own interest about how we shall use it or change it" (5). However, teaching students to resist the ideologies of genres can be difficult: when they use a genre, even in imitation in classroom settings, they are acting somewhat according to the ideology inherent in that genre. Heather Marie Bastian argues that "when we perform genres, we are positioned not only as situation-specific genre subjects but also [as] an overarching generic subject. And both of these positionings work to create complacent subjects" (7). By performing genres, then, students may not later be able to resist the ideologies of those genres.

As we can see, these are the characteristics of genre: social, rhetorical, dynamic, historical, cultural, situated, and ideological. Different theories about genre place varying degrees of emphasis on these characteristics, and doing this results in different views of what it means to use or learn a genre. Those differences are the foundation for and the results of the range of genre theories.

GENRE THEORIES

Traditional genre theory, as explained earlier, deals with customary definitions of genre: literary, form-focused, and fixed. More recent rhetorical genre theory focuses on (1) everyday, workplace, or school texts; (2) situation and context as they relate to textual regularities; (3) the dynamic, fluid nature of genres; (4) the blurring of boundaries; and (5) the ways genres develop from other genres. In contrast to traditional genre theory, this contemporary notion of genre theory recognizes genres as ideological and conceptual rather than neutral and concrete. Freedman and Medway also observe that contemporary genre theory is "descriptive, rather than prescriptive" ("Introduction" 3).

Within this broad generalization of contemporary genre theory, though, are a range of theories that differ on the various implications of genre concepts. Some of this difference has to do with place: theories that developed out of the Australian linguistic foundation have different concerns and theoretical origins than do those that developed out of the North American foundation. As Coe notes, "genre theories vary significantly" because they "are themselves motivated and situated" ("New Rhetoric" 198). In Australia, concerns with helping marginalized groups gain access to the social and economic mainstream were addressed by linguists looking for application of their ideas in schools. Widespread dissatisfaction with the more expressivist aspects of the writing process movement there influenced an approach to genre that emphasized practical aspects, including form. In contrast, in the United States, where the writing process movement had very strong support, rhetoricians' interests in the social aspects of writing were more theoretical than practical. So although similar issues were at play in both regions, those stressed in Australia were not as vital in the United States. As a result, the differing

Concrete		Abstract
Genre as ... Text	Rhetoric	Practice

Figure 1. The Genre Theory Continuum

needs and input created different tangents for the direction of genre theory. What eventually developed among theorists across the world was a range of ideas for what genre theory really is: genre theories—plural.

Bazerman and Prior summarize the range of genre theories in this way: "Genre has been explored in recent decades from three quite different perspectives: as text, as rhetoric, and as practice" ("Participating" 138). As I interpret their summary, we could look at these different theoretical perspectives along a continuum, with *genre as text* as the most concrete theory and *genre as practice* as the most abstract. Theorists with these various perspectives emphasize different elements of common aspects of theory (Figure 1).

Genre as Text

Genre theories at one end of the continuum, *genre as text*, tend toward a formalist perspective. Although theorists look at the ways the features of the form reflect the social situation, they generally begin with the form. Thus, from this perspective, résumés put important information in prominent positions grouped under common headings—education, experience, references—and in noticeable styles because the audience is usually a busy professional looking quickly through a number of documents. Despite an understanding of the relationship between context and text, though, there is a tendency for those with this perspective to emphasize form more than situation.

This theoretical position, genre as text, depends on a somewhat traditional concept of genre—stable, though still responsive to context—since this point of view "rest[s] not on what a genre is . . . but on how genres are textually realized" (Bazerman and Prior, "Participating" 138). Instruction in genres often stems from this theoretical position. Because instructional plans in classrooms remove most genres from actual contexts and must rely on the stability of genres for teaching, forms are an obvious *what's left*. A major goal for many in the genre as text group is to help marginalized groups find ways into the roles of power: if a person can't write a business letter, how likely is that person to get a job that will allow her to move into circles of influence? This goal explains a pedagogical inclination toward focusing on textual features: students would need fairly stable models and instruction in formal features to help them learn the genres.

However, Freedman and Medway note that providing equal access isn't as simple as teaching the forms of genres: "Students from nondominant positions cannot become powerful by simply adopting the genres of power, since the latter embody values and assumptions opposed to those held by people outside the centres of power" ("Introduction" 15). Students have to act and be what the genres represent, not just copy the forms, to assume an insider position. And even if all it took to become part of the powerful was to adopt the forms of that culture, Kress stresses another problem with this theoretical position: "The emphasis on access to the genres of power would lead to a spurious kind of equity, in which there was no challenge to the existing status quo of social arrangements" ("Genre and the Changing Contexts" 464). In other words, students might be able to join the community but might never be aware of the ideological implications of that association. Also, the genre as text perspective may diminish students' understanding of the dynamic aspect of genre and fail to acknowledge genres' full complexity. Too much focus on form might suggest that genres are formulaic and might not provide students with a sense that users have options that can reflect situations and individual needs within those situations.

Genre as Rhetoric

Theorists in the more central position, *genre as rhetoric,* emphasize the social actions that give rise to a genre. Because certain situations have developed forms for acting in those situations, for these theorists, genres are ways of acting: "Writing is not only a skill; it is also a way of being and acting in the world at a particular time, in a particular situation, for the achievement of particular desires" (Bawarshi, *Genre* 156). As Bazerman and Prior explain it, this theoretical position "stays focused on textual features, but reads those features as parts of a sociorhetorical situation" ("Participating" 138). Visible textual features are seen as perspectives *into* a situation, not as ends in themselves. These theorists might begin with the text but move into a consideration of the ways the texts they explore both respond to situations and allow for variety and change in those situations. If forms arise from context, using those forms as a way to look back at the context seems logical, as Joseph M. Williams and

Gregory G. Colomb assert: "When we learn social context, we are also learning its forms; but when we learn forms, we may also be learning their social contexts" (262). From this perspective, writing isn't only, or even primarily, about the text anymore; it's also about the situation surrounding the writing, about understanding that situation, and about ensuring that the rhetorical choices made in using a genre are effective for the situation and the user.

Devitt notes limitations to this perspective, though: "Interpreting discourse features thus requires not only situational but also cultural astuteness. . . . It is difficult for those who have not acted through the genres to recognize the full meaning and significance of textual features" (*Writing* 53). Thus, when texts are considered in relation to context, all the values and ideologies inherent in the culture and situation might not be visible to outsiders who look at the text alone.

Genre as Practice

The third perspective, *genre as practice*, begins "with the process of making genres" rather than with the genres themselves (Bazerman and Prior, "Participating" 139). Theorists in this range see "textual practices as fundamental to generic action" and emphasize the "dynamic, fluid, heterogeneous, and situated" aspects of genres (138). These theorists focus more on the contexts and processes related to genre *use* than on the genres themselves, or they see genres as actions, ways of being, rather than texts. Because those with this perspective emphasize the dynamic aspect of genres—their "fragility, plasticity, and heterogeneity" (139)—as central to genre theory, they are more likely to try to describe genre change in a particular setting and focus on the instability of genres than they are to look at a text as an artifact that would provide a lens into a situation or as a text that would represent a situation, as the other two perspectives do.

Theorists with this perspective rarely promote a pedagogical application of theory because "learning genres involves learning to act—with other people, artifacts, and environments, all of which are themselves in ongoing processes of change and development" (Bazerman and Prior, "Participating" 147). For these theorists, the focus is on the characteristics of genre interaction, on ways of creating meaning, on the actions genres enable. Not only can a genre be a way of making a text and a way of acting in a certain situation but it can also be a way to make sense of a situation, a way to view the world. Thus, this theoretical position emphasizes ideologies and perspectives, actions rather than texts.

THEORIES IN PRACTICE

Does it matter that theorists can't come to a single, unified theory about genres? Not really. In fact, our thinking and practice can be richer for this diversity of thought. What does matter is our understanding of how these various theories of genre play out in practice, of their possibilities and potential for student learning. The nature of the differences in theory results in very divergent views on what theory should look like in classrooms. *Mindful* teachers, to adapt Richard Fulkerson's use of Charles Silberman's term, know what theory is represented in their pedagogy.

The initial model proposed for instruction from the genre as text perspective established a three-part pattern: (1) examination of a model text, (2) followed by group imitation of the text, (3) leading to individual imitation of the text. The model was critiqued as too focused on form and on academic genres, thus stifling creativity and personal expression. This criticism came despite the assertion by J. R. Martin, Frances Christie, and Joan Rothery (the model's authors) years earlier that "it is very important to recognize that genres make meaning: they are not simply a set of formal structures into which meanings are poured" (64). In response to the criticism and as a result of dialogue among educators, the model was revised.

J. R. Martin's revised model presents a more contextualized interpretation of genre (128). It begins with students investigating the social context of a genre before they examine the genre (text) itself. To have students move away from seeing texts simply as forms, guiding questions for examining the text relate to functions and relationships, not only to formal features. After students practice independent construction of texts, they are encouraged to reflect on (and critique) the genre, questioning the ideas and relationships the genre privileges. The revised model, then, moves toward a more theoretically rich understanding of genre by having students investigate context *before* looking at sample texts and critique the genre *after* creating their own imitations.

The interest in equity exhibited by those who favor this theoretical position is admirable; the potential for focus on text forms, sometimes to the point of formulas, is less representative of genre theory than some theorists like. Given the first try at making this model work in classrooms and how formulaic it became, critics feel that the revised approach may still endorse a tendency, in some teachers' hands, to diminish the idea of genre until it's almost a fill-in-the-blank concept, especially if there is limited variety in the examples of the studied genre and a focus on replicating one example. However, when Julie E. Wollman-Bonilla observed teachers following a process similar to this model, she noted that the teachers "did not explicitly discuss grammatical choices" but rather modeled the grammatical and structural *options* in interactive writing with the students, thus moving away from teaching genres as formulas (41). Therefore, it seems that an approach based on genre as text may be highly dependent on each individual teacher's use of the instructional model and her understanding of theory as it informs practice.

The genre as rhetoric group looks at texts as responses to situations and thereby links the two aspects of genre theory that are most consistent among the different approaches—text and context. The method of instruction is less patterned than the genre as text's plan, but it generally involves examining a specific context, the people involved in that context, and the texts they use. Students analyze a variety of sample texts and ask questions about the noticeable features, not primarily to identify the features but more to determine how those features both reflect and respond to the situations the genres come from and to evaluate how effective the rhetorical choices might be in a particular situation. As Coe notes, this perspective of genre alters some basic conceptions about the teaching of writing; at the very least, he says, it should encourage writers to "recognize that different writing situations require different types of writing, that what is good in a piece of academic literary criticism may not be good in a newspaper book review and will very likely not be good in a brochure" ("New Rhetoric" 200). It should help students see how writing derives from and responds to situations that require action.

In some cases of practice from this theoretical perspective, students replicate the genres; in others the investigation of the relationship between text and context is the sole purpose of the questioning. Some theorists worry that this approach still focuses too much on the text, not allowing enough room for the change and variation that is part of genre theory, especially if the samples students investigate are too limited in number or too similar to each other. Other theorists wonder if it's really possible to see the whole situation from outside the context, just by looking at the text. They believe this method of exploration would provide a somewhat superficial sense of the situation and therefore a somewhat limited ability to determine rhetorical effectiveness.

The genre as practice group focuses most on the context and the dynamic nature of genres, to the point that some adherents assert that genres are impossible to teach in a classroom. Instead, proponents take an approach similar to Gee's applications of learned versus acquired literacy, in which he states that "someone cannot engage in a Discourse in a less than fully fluent manner. You are either in it or you're not. Discourses are connected with displays of an identity" (155). Applying this perspective to writing and writing instruction, Sidney I. Dobrin explains: "The systems by which we interpret are not codifiable in any logical manner since discourse does not operate in any logico-systemic manner and never remains static long enough to develop concrete understandings of the communicative interaction. In other words, there are no codifiable processes by which we can characterize, identify, solidify, grasp discourse, and, hence, there is no way to teach discourse, discourse interpretation, or discourse disruption" (132–33).

Theorists from other theoretical positions (genre as text and genre as rhetoric) might question the value of the theory if it can't have an impact in educating students in writing and reading, although Dobrin defends that, too: "Classroom application need not always be the measure for value of theory" (133). Still, teachers might wonder how to prepare students for writing outside of school if there is no way to replicate situational contexts in classes and therefore no way to teach about genres until students encounter them on their own. Some theorists at this end of the continuum recommend, instead, teaching awareness of genres "to inculcate *receptive* skills . . . turn[ing] away from developing rhetorical skills and toward development of rhetorical sensibilities" (Petraglia 62). Thus, teachers with this perspective might be more likely to teach about context than about texts. Those with other theoretical perspectives and social agendas might find such an approach an evasion of the hard work of teaching writing as well as a route to reduced opportunities for equity.

In a very general way, this is an overview of contemporary genre theory and its uses in the classroom. Like the tip of an iceberg, there is more complexity and detail to the theory than is presented here. A passage in Devitt's book hints at the depth of thinking that has occurred, is occurring, and will occur related to genre theory: "Many areas of genre theory still need further research and exploration. For example, not all genres allow a simple matchup with a particular set of contexts; some might interact with multiple contexts. Not all contexts that people define as recurring produce recognized genres, and some may produce more than one genre. People may, of course, mix genres and mix contexts, and they may use genres badly. Genres may be unsuccessful, fail, or die out. Genre is too rich a subject to be mined completely in just one volume" (*Writing* 31). With these words, Devitt acknowledges some of the questions still to be addressed by theorists. In the appendixes, I address some additional questions and issues related to genre theory. In an effort to address some of the concerns Devitt mentions, I also explain a little more about some of the new directions in which genre theory is moving.

3 Pedagogical Challenges and Principles

CHALLENGES

As I've already indicated, there are obvious difficulties in translating genre theory into classroom practice. As Ann M. Johns points out, "there are direct contradictions between what the theoreticians and researchers continue to discover about the nature of genres and the everyday requirements of the classroom" ("Destabilizing" 237). In addition to a common apprehension that a genre approach will emphasize form and neglect the social action of a genre, we can add that trying to infer the social context from the genre, a way to move beyond forms, is also possibly problematic.

Additionally, there are questions about whether genres can be taught in schools at all because they would occur out of their normal context. Freedman and Medway address this constraint to pedagogy: "School writing may imitate and adapt features of working genres but cannot be those genres; it is doomed, whatever its transparent features, to remain school writing, a solution to a quite different set of exigencies" ("Introduction" 13–14). Given the current understanding about genres, it is expected that many theorists would claim that it is not possible to teach them in school because such instruction occurs away from "real" contexts. Reiff refers to Freedman and David Bleich, who both feel "that genres—like all language use—are not eligible for study once they are considered to be independent of their contexts of use" (Devitt, Bawarshi, and Reiff 553). David F. Kaufer and Cheryl Geisler seem to agree when they posit that "one must wonder how students ever grasp what it means to be an insider when their practice remains on the outside" (306). They acknowledge that students may learn conventions, although they believe those are also better learned in context, but they assert that the "tacit beliefs" necessary to act with genres can't be learned outside of their context (306).

Because of decontextualization, critics worry that all that will be left for instruction is the forms of genres, an emphasis that misses the point of genre theory altogether. Freedman and Medway stress this point: "According to our new, more rhetorically informed view, however, producing an example of a genre is a matter not just of generating a text with certain formal characteristics but of using generic resources to act effectively on a situation through a text" ("Introduction" 11). They add that knowing the formal characteristics of a genre is simple in comparison to doing the real work genres do. The hard part is that teaching genres in school is often teaching them out of context, therefore increasing a tendency to focus on formal properties of texts. Anne Herrington and Charles Moran note this problem in their review of writing textbooks that claim a genre focus. Their review shows that, "despite their attempts to construe genre as rhetorical action, [these textbooks] too often slide toward a representation of genre as decontextualized form" (15). They refer to Alan Luke's use of the term "freeze-drying" (15) to describe the way genres are often approached in schools, an approach that negates genres' dynamic, responsive character by limiting students' exposure to a few models shown in class. Teachers who use a genre approach would have to be very conscious of this tendency and watchful to avoid it.

Balancing instruction with implicit learning about genres seems to be the approach some theorists prefer. Mary Soliday describes the balance in this way:

> Bakhtin's theory suggests that if we want to help writers assimilate genre, we must remain aware of the dynamic between the individual writer's intentions and the constraints of form. In composition, two approaches to genre reflect this dynamic: explicit knowing, which reflects a community's traditions or expectations, and implicit knowing, which reflects how individuals meet those expectations. In my view the first approach includes making tacit knowledge explicit by designing rubrics, describing the purposes of form, and providing maps of textual features such as annotated models. Though of course these approaches will overlap, in general implicit learning includes modeling genre through class talk, offering regular feedback, and sequencing assignments. (79–80)

From this perspective, then, some of what teachers do explicitly in the classroom may enhance implicit learning about genres in actual situations where students find themselves because it builds awareness of genre difference and of some ways that genres act in different situations.

Arguing that an understanding of genre takes more than simply being in the presence of genres, Bazerman asserts that "going to the place [the genre's space] is only the first step, for once you are there you need access and encouragement to engage with particular people in particular roles, use particular resources, and take part in particular experiences and activities" ("Genre and Identity" 14). Although he might call it socialization instead of instruction, he also seems to suggest that some understanding of how to observe, how to make sense of a situation, and how to act are essential to learning genres—and these skills could be developed in schools, through instruction and practice.

Ways to help students gain these understandings could be learned outside a particular situation, as Gee suggests in his claims about literacy learning. First, he differentiates between learning and acquisition, noting that acquisition occurs in context and learning occurs in school. He claims that we are better at performing what we acquire, but we are better at explaining what we learn. Although he argues for literacy as largely acquired rather than learned, he recommends that students practice "mushfake Discourse"—what sounds like pretend genres (159). He explains *mushfake* as a prison term that means "to make do with something less when the real thing is not available. . . . I propose that we ought to produce 'mushfaking', resisting students, full of meta-knowledge" (159). In other words, he suggests that, in school, students learn aspects of genres such as language and form (a kind of genre as text) through practice with strategies and reflection so that they understand the concepts related to genres, even though they are not situated in actual contexts where those genres act. With such an approach, students can be prepared through instruction to interact with genres in authentic situations outside of school. Certainly his proposal has some merit because it addresses issues related to artificial contexts and transfer.

To address the issue of lack of context from another perspective, some theorists assert that school is itself a social setting and therefore a viable context for learning about genres—school genres, in particular. From the school context, students can gain genre experience that will provide an awareness of genres that is transferable to genre understanding outside of the classroom. Bazerman addresses this perspective when he asserts that school is a real social setting that allows for generic activity: "We have started to see how the classroom is a particular scene of writing—neither an innately natural nor an innately artificial scene; neither necessarily an oppressive nor necessarily a liberating scene; just a scene of writing" ("Where" 26). Bawarshi builds on this argument when he speaks of first-year writing (FYW) courses, although his argument can be made for most writing classrooms: "Seen in this light, the FYW course is not as artificial as some critics make it out to be. . . . The classroom in its own right is a dynamic, textured site of action mediated by a range of complex written and spoken genres that constitute student-teacher positions, relations, and practices" (*Genre* 118). Contemporary genre theory has complicated some aspects of genre for the classroom, but it has also opened some up because it helps us see the classroom as a site of action, capable of generic activity.

Since most approaches to genre involve using samples as part of the investigation, another problem raised in genre instruction is critics' concern that writing will be replaced by reading in the classroom, thereby undoing the emphasis on student writing gained in the last few decades. Furthermore, process advocates contend that reading a product cannot give writers an understanding of process and may even inhibit writing development as students look to the samples as rigid forms or as "too perfect" to even be attempted. Certainly these are valid concerns that teachers would need to address when implementing a genre approach in the classroom.

Despite these challenges, what genre theory can teach students about using language is too important to give up. Freedman and Medway, despite their concerns about the lack of context, acknowledge that there is some benefit in using a genre approach in schools when they assert that it can "grant experience of the ways of thinking or procedures for handling concepts and styles of deployment of argument that are employed in the professional domain" ("Introduction" 14). Genre theory can give us a new perspective for teaching writing. By carefully employing a genre approach in our writing instruction, we can improve our work with students and their success in using writing for their own purposes.

PRINCIPLES

As Devitt notes, "the teaching of genres . . . must develop thoughtfully, critically, and with recognition of the complexity, benefits, and dangers of the concept of genre" (*Writing* 191). Since most approaches to teaching will probably fall short of theory in some respect, keeping some guiding principles in mind may help us avoid the worst of the pitfalls and help us remember, as Johns counsels, that there is not "one 'true way' to approach genre theory or practice" (Preface i). Because of the challenges in teaching genres in classrooms, I offer the following principles to guide that instruction in ways that will most benefit students in acquiring the attitudes and abilities needed to write and use genres effectively.

Connection

Freedman notes that "interaction is at the heart of the genre" ("Situating" 180). Because of that, a key instructional principle must be keeping genre and context as connected as possible. According to Johns, separating texts from contexts reduces them to "artifacts for study rather than tools for achieving 'repeated social action' (Miller, 1984)" ("Destabilizing" 239). Devitt lists several reasons for keeping them connected: "Generic forms must be embedded within their social and rhetorical purposes so that rhetorical understanding can counter the urge toward formula. Genres must be embedded within their social and cultural ideologies so that critical awareness can counter potential ideological effects" (*Writing* 191). So, teachers need to keep context and text connected to help students avoid seeing genre as formula and for them to gain critical awareness. We might also add that the connection can help students see genres as ways to act, not just ways to write.

Some theorists suggest using texts as a way into context. With this approach, teachers help students notice the features that recur regularly through multiple samples of a genre. Once they have noticed the features, students speculate as to what the features might respond to or what they might accomplish for the users. Thus, students anticipate the social purposes and connect those purposes to textual features. Some of the potential limitations of this approach have been mentioned earlier. One is that it can be difficult to see contextual connections—and some theorists suggest that it is almost impossible, as Freedman implies when she poses these questions: "If the textual features are secondary to the prior communicative purpose, is there any value in explicating these textual features out of context as a way of teaching the genre? Or, if genres are responses to contexts, can they be learned out of context by explicating features and specifying rules of either form or context?" ("Show" 225). However, inferring context from text can be constrained by our experience. If students' experience is limited, this inferred connection from text to context may take extra effort for them to discover.

Another challenge with this approach is that it can be very hard to identify ideology. For instance, many instructors teach students about résumés, and students learn the general aspects of the form. Students may recognize how the features respond to a social situation—a busy reader who wants to gather information specific to the situation quickly—but as T. Shane Peagler and Kathleen Blake Yancey point out, students often don't see résumés as "written in the context of any rhetorical situation" (154). As Devitt, Reiff, and Bawarshi report, Randall Popken has identified the ideological aspect of résumés that students may not notice so easily from the "subjectless sentences," the "physical constraints," and the "prescribed categories" (*Scenes* 159–60): "By downplaying the voice and persona of résumé writers, the résumé depersonalizes job seekers, portraying them as commodities that can be sold" (159). Students also need to identify ideologies so that they can learn to critique a genre and make the most effective connections between text and context. This may be more difficult than it seems.

Instead of looking first at texts and through them to contexts, Devitt, Reiff, and Bawarshi, in *Scenes of Writing: Strategies for Composing with Genres,* propose a reverse order to ensure connection between text and context: "Teach students to move from observation of the writing scene and its shared goals, to the rhetorical interactions that make up the situations of this scene (the readers, writers, purposes, subjects, and settings), to the genres used to participate within the situations and scenes" (xviii). In their approach, Devitt, Reiff, and Bawarshi provide guided analysis to help students analyze situations and the genres within them. In this way, they hope that students are better able to see any genre as embedded in a situation rather than separate from it. Certainly there is still, will always be, the possibility of reducing genres to textual forms; however, the intent is that starting with context first will minimize that tendency. Part of this approach also includes critiquing genres, with questions (including the following) as ways to help students accomplish this important task of trying to see the ideologies of genres, too:

- What does the genre allow its users to do and what does it not allow them to do?
- Whose needs are most served by the genre? Whose needs are least served?
- Does the genre enable its users to represent themselves fully?
- Do the assumptions that the genre reflects privilege certain ways of doing things?
- Does the genre allow its users to do certain things at the expense of others? And if so, at what cost? (161)

By beginning with the context and including specific ways to address ideology, this approach works at keeping genres and context connected effectively.

Pang reports on a study comparing the two approaches: one beginning with texts to determine their features and, from them, their functions in the context, and the other looking at a context first and then at the texts that grow out of it. To uncover which approach would give students the best strategy for future use with genres they didn't know, students from each approach explored other genres and were asked to determine the "possible discourse purposes underlying each genre and to select moves appropriate for each purpose" (152). The results? "Both approaches yielded almost equal results in the quality of the subjects' writing products and their use of strategies to compose" (158). Pang acknowledges some key features of the teaching in both approaches that he sees as contributing to the finding: "Both approaches in the study avoid the learning of formulae. Instead, learners were encouraged to formulate their own 'rules.' Above all, learners needed to familiarize themselves with the idea of choice, of making choices based on informed judgments of the wider sociocultural context, and identifying the interpersonal, ideational/experiential, and textual variables in the immediate situation of communication" (158). We can conclude that either approach—starting with texts or starting with contexts—can benefit students as genre users if the teacher keeps text and context connected, resists students' inclinations to look at genres simplistically (as forms), and helps students see genres as both social and individual.

Other theorists recommend using genres in the context of the classroom as a way to make an authentic connection between genres and situation. Under this proposed course of action, teachers would help students see the situation that exists in schools and classrooms, the actions school writing is meant to accomplish, and the roles students are expected to assume for writing in those situations—including testing. With these understandings, students could then make better choices from the range of rhetorical options available to them for each kind of writing. For example, teachers could have students use genres in the classroom to accomplish classroom tasks, such as writing memos requesting procedural changes in the classroom. Teachers could also have students use genres to conduct schoolwork that connects to the world outside the classroom, such as writing letters for information they need or conducting interviews for research. Students could also conduct mini-ethnographies, since these use genre analysis to create a genre. With any of these methods, the situation and the genre are connected through actual practice that allows students to act within the classroom context.

Despite her own preferences, Devitt asserts that her "point is not to argue for a particular pedagogical strategy as much as to argue for pedagogical strategies that keep generic form and generic contexts united" (*Writing* 200). However we can keep them together—through sequencing or through making authentic texts in the classroom—connection is key to effective instruction.

Creativity

When it comes to teaching genre, an important principle should be teaching genres "as both constraint and choice so that individual awareness can lead to individual creativity" (Devitt, *Writing* 191). One issue raised about a genre approach is that it could limit writers' creativity through a focus on either the forms or the social aspect of genres. Devitt addresses this concern with an attention to balance:

> Research on creativity helps us, too, with how to teach students to be both communicative and creative. Writers need both convergence and divergence. . . . Students need to learn how to make their texts fit within the patternings of converging situations and texts; they also need to learn how to diverge from those patternings in order to say what they want to say. Both kinds of learning are learning about genre. Both kinds of learning are necessary to encourage students' creativity. Both kinds of learning can also enable students to critique the social values, assumptions, and beliefs that have shaped those patternings, those genres. Helping students discover the rhetorical and social strategies behind the forms, their purposes and effects, what conformity they allow and what choices they require can develop students' critical as well as creative abilities. (*Writing* 156)

One way teachers address creativity in teaching genres is to begin with the belief that genres offer options as much as—or more than—they do limitations. In their work with teachers from several countries, Heather Kay and Tony Dudley-Evans found reservations "that the genre-based approach is restrictive, especially in the hands of unimaginative teachers" (311). "Unimaginative" teachers would be those who don't see that, as William Strong phrases it, a genre "has fixed conventions, but it also has flexible slots" (163). With that concern in mind, teachers should approach genres differently, as flexible forms, rather than representing them as fixed structures. Even with this understanding, it is still possible for students to interpret genres as rule bound, as Peagler and Yancey note (160). However, with a descriptive, rather than prescriptive, teacher stance, students are more likely to develop appropriate perspectives about genres and creativity.

The use of samples or exemplars is one way teachers can help students see creativity and flexibility in genres. As Devitt explains, it "seems clear from all research that writers need to be familiar with a genre to write it well" (*Writing* 209). Using samples is important, but there are problems when teachers use models limited either in breadth or in number. Courtney B. Cazden gives an example of an Australian woman who as a child had learned about only "wooley white sheep" in school. When she saw brown sheep, she didn't know what they were: "I fear that identification of sheep with whiteness exemplifies the dangers of impoverished, stereotyped, and therefore inflexible concepts that are too often the outcomes of our teaching, including—of most relevance here—the teaching of genres" (7). The potential pitfalls of using limited samples should be clear from this example: we don't want students to view genres through such a narrow perspective.

An obvious way to help students avoid looking at samples as formulas is to provide a broad variety of them—as Devitt says, "as wide a range of samples as possible, ones reflecting different uses of language and form even while achieving similar purposes in similar settings" (*Writing* 200). With an array of samples, teachers can encourage students to focus on their diverse nature. We have a tendency to look for similarities naturally, so emphasizing variety will reinforce the flexibility of genres. Similarly, Chapman recommends asking students to "deconstruct and reconstruct [genres] to understand and own them. In this way, the use of models may be process oriented (to foster genre awareness) rather than product oriented (to produce a piece of writing that adheres to a particular set of conventions)" (488). Looking for the variety themselves can reinforce students' understanding of genres as flexible and responsive to situation.

Nevertheless, even when teachers use multiple samples, problems with this approach don't disappear. Devitt finds that "students easily turn samples into models, and models easily turn writing into formula. . . . Even given a range of samples of a genre, writers might well narrow their view to a single text, which they may then treat as a prototype or exemplar of that genre" (*Writing* 209). Despite this potential hazard, though, using samples is better than not using them: "To ask students to write new genres with no samples of those genres is to reduce their learning by increasing their anxiety" (209). Mary Ehrenworth and Vicki Vinton try to avoid potential problems by referring to samples as "mentor texts" rather than models (129). A shift in vocabulary—using the word *mentor*, suggesting a guide or advisor, as opposed to *model*, which implies a pattern to be followed—might enable students to move away from reducing sample texts to forms and toward seeing them as options.

Teachers also encourage creativity when they ask students to consider the purposes behind the options they find in the samples. Students may not be right in their guesses, but they will still be learning to think about situations and rhetorical choices and how they could connect. Anne Herrington and Charles Moran assert that the exploration of possible purposes should involve a "good deal of interaction and negotiation wherein students' views are respected: interactions between teacher and students, between student and students, and between reading and writing" (252). Repeatedly theorists and researchers acknowledge the value of rich discourse in classes using a genre approach. Giving students opportunities to talk about genres aids their learning and supports the social aspect of genre instruction: they can see and question choices and their effects on others in the classroom. Such talk will also allow students to explore how far they can stretch a genre's boundaries: When does it become another genre? What are the effects of those boundary-stretching choices? Such classroom discourse enhances the concept of creativity in relation to genres.

When teachers make sure students see flexibility in genres, they should not then undermine that progress by using grading criteria that are so narrowly focused that flexibility is actually discouraged or so broadly stated that they could apply to any piece of writing. Instead of advocating what he calls "all-purpose criteria," Charles R. Cooper recommends instead "genre-specific criteria, which are particularly helpful as guidelines for the writer, for peer critique, and for self-evaluation" (31). When creating genre-specific criteria, to avoid a too-narrow focus, Devitt urges teachers to use criteria "described in terms of their purposes and settings" rather than features of form (*Writing* 208). So, instead of asking for five adjectives to establish setting in the introductory paragraph, the rubric could ask for adequate details so that the reader can visualize the setting of a personal narrative. Since students are as likely to use assessment criteria as other aspects of the class in refining their understanding of genre, it is particularly important that we develop genre-specific criteria that teach about genres but still allow room for creativity and individuality.

Rhetoric

Many of our students harbor the misconception that writing well in one situation requires the same strategies and actions as writing well in another situation. But genres are rhetorical: "Rhetoric is the use of language to accomplish something, and rhetorical choices are the decisions speakers and writers make in order to accomplish something with language" (Devitt, Reiff, and Bawarshi 6). A genre approach is rhetorical because it pays attention to the situation and the strategies unique to each communicative action. As David Foster explains, "writing becomes a meaningful event, in this view, not because the writer follows the right steps in producing the text, but because she reads the situation and the reader accurately and finds ways to adapt her language to the contingent requirements of the writing moment" (153). Good writing, therefore, is rhetorical *and* situated. Whether it's good depends on its context and how effectively it does its job in that context. Devitt, Reiff, and Bawarshi suggest that the following choices are rhetorical:

> What sort of tone and language to use;
> How to engage and address others;
> How to develop, organize, and present one's ideas so that others
> can relate to them;
> What kinds of examples to use when communicating;
> When and how to start talking and when and how to stop. (6)

They assert that "the more appropriate your rhetorical choices, the more likely you are to communicate effectively" (6). Effective action with genres depends on appropriate rhetorical choices.

Coe explains that "the proper first step for preparing to teach a particular genre is often to locate it in rhetorical situation and context of situation" ("Teaching" 161). Students should consider the relationship they are establishing and the situational aspects that come to bear on the relationship that show up in the writing. To do this, Coe recommends "that each piece of writing have a specifically defined rhetorical situation which may be stipulated by the assignment or the student" (162). Then, for each assignment, students include on the title page the rhetorical context—purpose, audience, occasion (genre)—and the teacher assesses the paper on how well it addresses its designated context (162).

Rhetorical writing includes being strategic because it involves writers making choices dependent upon their goals. Those choices are intentional, planned, tactical. They respond to audience, to purpose, to situation, and to genre. Being rhetorical and strategic, Joseph J. Comprone suggests, can support an important aspect of a genre approach: "This emphasis on developing strategies to guide choice making in the process of producing written text can become the theoretical basis for introducing rhetorical technique and method into writing courses; it can also become a way of developing an approach to literacy through which the mediation of socially constructed genres and individual choice making within particular textual situations can be accomplished" (102). The idea of developing students' abilities to see writing as making choices is particularly important. A genre approach must include making rhetorical choices strategically, because genres respond to varying situations and writers act with them.

Reflection

Peter Smagorinsky and Michael W. Smith encourage the "mindful attention to transfer—that is the conscious and deliberate application of knowledge in contexts other than the one originally studied" (291). Because teachers cannot teach all genres students will ever need to know, it is important that genre knowledge acquired from the genres used in class-rooms transfer to other genre situations students act in. That transfer occurs through metacognitive processing—reflection—that takes place when students contemplate "a genre and one's own positioning using that genre" (Herrington and Moran 252). Smagorinsky and Smith, citing research by D. N. Perkins and Gavriel Salomon, also assert that "teach-ers who 'persistently and systematically . . . saturate the context of edu-cation with attention to transfer' (p. 29) will improve the likelihood that students will reapply the knowledge when they shift domains" (291). Reflection provides a place for students to articulate understanding, thereby enhancing the chances for transfer of learning.

Carl Nagin, in *Because Writing Matters: Improving Student Writing in Our Schools,* observes that "to develop as writers, students also need the opportunity to articulate their own awareness and understanding of their processes in learning to write. Research has shown the importance of such metacognitive thinking in becoming a better writer" (National Writing Project 82). Yancey also sees reflection as an important part of writers' development when she concludes that "over time . . . reflection provides the ground where the writer invents, repeatedly and recursively, a composing self. Concurrently, reflection contributes to the writing of texts that themselves are marked by reflective tenor—multi-contextual, thoughtful, holistic" (200). These findings seem to suggest that the kind of writer who has the ability to be and practices being reflective is the kind of writer who will be sensitive to genre, to situation, to context, and to relationships established through genres. Reflection may even be a necessity to help students resist seeing genres as forms and recognize ideologies as well.

Yancey, in addressing the genres students use to reflect, observes that those genres are as important as the genres they reflect on: "If the point, ultimately, of reflection is to encourage reflective writers, and if we expect those writers to work in various genres, then it might make sense to ask for more than one kind of reflective text" (154). She proposes cover letters, individual annotations, or "final reflective essay[s]" in their portfolios (69), Talk-To's and Talk-Backs (108), or a number of other genres varying in formality that students can use to respond to their own writ-ing. Any of these would be valuable components of a genre approach because they help students look more critically not only at their own generic responses but also at the situations in which they occur and the relationships and roles they acknowledge or don't. Such reflection moves students' work with genres beyond the level of an "assignment" that they complete and turn in to a part of their overall learning and development as writers and as actors in social situations.

Smagorinsky and Smith note that for reflection to be effective, it needs to be "an integral part of the class structure rather than a tag at the end of a lesson; [Gavriel] Salomon (1987) has found that most students are decidedly unmindful unless specifically and vigorously cued" (291). Yancey makes the same point about the need to make reflection an integral part of the writing classroom: "For reflection to be generative and constructive . . . it must be practiced, must itself be woven not so much throughout the curricula as *into* it" (201). These are powerful reminders that the reflective attitude is an integral part of a genre approach because of the need to consider all writing as social and situated. Reflection is that and does that.

CHOOSING GENRES

The choice of genres for classroom exploration is of singular importance. First, as Devitt reminds us, "whatever genres are taught will also entail not teaching others" (*Writing* 206). Choosing some genres means, by necessity, leaving others out. Additionally, since genres provide ways of viewing the world, the genres we select favor and develop certain perspectives more than others. Repeatedly selecting five-paragraph essays promotes logic and distance. Repeatedly selecting personal narratives promotes individual and chronological perspectives. Consistently choosing work-related genres shows a valuing of one worldview, while consistently choosing poetry shows another.

So, how do we pick? Heather Lattimer selects genres for classroom study by looking first at state and district standards. Sometimes these standards include textual descriptions like informational text or personal narrative. Within such broad categories—what William Grabe calls macro-genres (252) and Vijay K. Bhatia calls genre colonies (280)—Lattimer selects genres such as memoir or feature article. She warns "against choosing genre studies that are too broadly or too narrowly defined," such as "nonfiction," because the category "quickly becomes unwieldy" (8). She also considers students' future use of a genre, especially public use—what she calls "authenticity" (9). Coe also suggests choosing on the basis of students' future needs: genres students will be motivated to learn (such as college entrance essays) and ones teaching patterns of thinking that students will need (analysis, for example) (Johns et al. 246). The goals of the course and the students' experiences with genres are also important determining factors in the selection process. Devitt proposes, as one option, that teachers find genres that overlap with those students have already encountered, so that students can "draw on known genres to tackle unfamiliar situations" (*Writing* 207). Chapman supports Devitt's approach because "current thinking suggests that we learn new genres by forming analogies and making connections with the ones we already know" (472). When we do select genres that build on students' current genre knowledge, however, we should also ensure that the genres we introduce offer a variety, allowing students to see ways that genres are alike and ways that they differ. Such variety will develop their awareness of genres.

Selecting carefully, keeping in mind the course, the students, and the contexts of the genres, will help students gain exposure to the genres that will be most beneficial to them in the long term. No schooling can possibly address all the genres a person will act with throughout a lifetime: schools don't have the time and teachers don't have the prescience to see the future of each student in the classroom. Instead, teachers should select with the idea of creating the best foundation of genre understanding possible—what Devitt calls antecedent genres: "The criteria for choosing genres should include which genres best supplement students' existing genre repertoires and may serve as especially rich antecedent genres" (*Writing* 203).

Antecedent genres are those genres we understand from prior experience that come to bear on current genre experience. As Bazerman explains it, "when we travel to new communicative domains, we construct our perception of them beginning with the forms we know" ("The Life" 19). Judith A. Langer's research with young children confirms the influence of antecedent genres: "The functional forms [children] hear and use in their daily lives serve as their models" (185). Jamieson's study of inaugural addresses makes this point too: "rhetors do perceive unprecedented situations through antecedent genres" (414). If students use the genres they know to act in new situations, then selecting genres to teach is important for providing the best foundation for future genre acquisition and learning. As Devitt points out, "individuals can only draw from genres they know. . . . The more genres they know, the more potential antecedent genres they have for addressing new situations" (*Writing* 204). Teachers' choices and use of genres can have an important impact on students' futures. We need to ensure that the genres studied or used in classes provide rich antecedent genres for students' future experience with genres.

Despite the identified need to expose students to many genres, Devitt notes that "not all genres serve as equally appropriate or equally helpful . . . antecedents" (*Writing* 206). Lattimer avoids diaries in a genre study for this reason: for her, they are not beneficial as an antecedent genre because they are not representative of the genres adults use to interact with others. Rich antecedents would be those that have more carryover with other genres and that are used more regularly in social interactions.

However, simply having exposure to genres or using them isn't all that influences students' appropriate use of genre knowledge in the future. They also have to learn to choose from their antecedent knowledge appropriately. As Jamieson's study shows, "the antecedent genres chosen may not be appropriate to the situation" (414). Teachers confront this problem with selection when their students use language from commercials to write persuasion or summarize a story instead of analyzing it. Because of this inappropriate use of antecedents, students need to understand genres from a contextual and ideological perspective as well as from a textual one. If they are aware of the contexts and purposes and audiences for a particular genre, they will be more likely to choose appropriately from their genre repertoire when they face a new situation.

Many factors influence our choices of which genres to teach. And those choices are important. Still, whatever we select, we should also remember Coe's admonition that "developing an awareness that different situations call for writing in different genres is far more important than learning any particular genre" (Johns et al. 247). That's something a genre approach can help us do.

The teaching ideas that follow attempt to address key concepts of genre theory in the best way possible for the secondary-level classroom. I acknowledge that not all applications will be appreciated by all genre theorists, however. These applications address genre as text and genre as rhetoric, as well as concepts about genre that might satisfy those at the genre as practice end of the continuum.

II Practice

Once students learn what it is to engage deeply and write well in any particular circumstance, they have a sense of the possibilities of literate participation in any discursive arena.

Charles Bazerman, "The Life of Genre, the Life in the Classroom"

4 Teaching Genre Concepts

DISCOVERING GENRES

Even if we can't develop the full contextual aspect of some genres because of the restrictions of the classroom situation, it is helpful for students to know that not all writing is the same. They can learn the *concept* of genres. To begin, it is important for them to know that "studying genre is studying how people use language to make their way in the world" (Devitt, *Writing* 9). By exploring their own uses of language and texts, students can see those uses in social interactions that constitute genres.

■ Begin this exploration by first helping students understand that not all writing is the same. Ask them to list what kinds of writing they feel they do well and what kinds they don't feel they do well. Discuss these lists in class. Such conversation allows us to acknowledge that we all write for different purposes and that all of us are good at some kinds of writing—and that all of us, including teachers, have kinds of writing that challenge us.

■ Cooper writes that genres "emerge from social interactions and the need to communicate" (25). Students should also understand this social aspect of genres. Have them generate a list, over several days, of the ways they use written language to accomplish different tasks. They need to consider all writing, not just school writing and not just writing on paper—they write on phones, on keyboards, with chalk or markers, even with their fingers (messages in the steam on a car window). After they have developed their lists, go over them as a class and create a master list. Encourage students to think of any more ways they use writing that they may have failed to list individually but that come to mind as they hear others' suggestions.

■ Have students break into small groups to discuss the master list and decide if any of the ways of writing are the same type, or genre, by using questions like these: What purposes do the different kinds of writing serve? Are any social contexts similar? If some seem to be the same "kind" of writing, have students group those together and discuss why they belong together. Devitt explains that David Russell "takes as a given that participants' recognition of a genre is what rightly determines whether one genre is distinct from another" (*Writing* 8). If what Russell says and Devitt endorses is true, then our students' sense of purpose and boundaries is valid. There really aren't right and wrong responses here so much as an exploration of what constitutes genre. So, students should, for example, consider in discussion if email and text messaging are different genres or not. If they are different, what makes them so? If they are not, how are they alike—what social purposes do they both serve? How are their situations similar? Does the technology matter (that is, can notes on paper be the same genre as a text message)?

- Since, as I've mentioned, "studying genre is studying how people use language to make their way in the world" (Devitt, *Writing* 9), students should examine the language of some genres they use. How does the language of specific genres fit their purpose and social context? If, for example, they decided that email messages to teachers or to businesses are the same genre as email messages to friends, what language differences might students find among them? Is that enough difference to say they are different genres? Why or why not?

- Further discussion could develop ideas about genres of business and genres of power. How do these differ from genres students use with friends or in casual situations? What are the consequences of responding inappropriately to the situation of a genre: in other words, if a student uses the language of a text message in a letter of application for a job, what are the potential consequences? Is the choice worth the potential problems? Have students discuss these issues as a way to clarify what genres are and what they mean to them in their daily lives.

- As a way to articulate the conclusions from the discussion and promote individual learning, end by having students write reflections about their personal definitions of each genre and how a knowledge of genre can be important.

BUILDING GENRE AWARENESS

An application that focuses on awareness more than acquisition is one way to address genre theory in the classroom. In early writing on post-process theory, Petraglia, agreeing with recommendations from Roderick Hart and Don Burks, urges the development of "*sensitivity* to the rhetorical possibilities available" (62): "not to improve students' writing skills but to make students informed consumers of written discourse in the hope that they may become better producers of it as well" (63). Because it begins with the idea that there is no one right way to write, an awareness approach helps students learn to adjust language to situation.

An awareness approach leans more to the genre as practice end of the continuum because it focuses less on genres themselves and more on what genres mean, how they respond to context, and how they represent ways of viewing and valuing the world. Devitt explains that an awareness approach teaches writers how to consider new genres, because it gives them strategies for and practice with examining samples of genres and then knowing "how to interpret what they find, especially discerning the required from the optional elements and the rhetorical nature of the genre, to understand its context and functions for its users, in order to avoid formulaic copying of a model" (*Writing* 201).

The following application is based on ideas from *Scenes of Writing* by Devitt, Reiff, and Bawarshi (93–94).

■ Choose a genre to use for class investigation and have students explore its context, or what Devitt and her colleagues call the scene and situation. The authors use the terms *scene* to correspond to the larger context and *situation* to refer to the immediate context of a genre. For example, if our class were going to investigate the genre of want ads to sell cars, the scene could include a newspaper, a website, or booklets found outside fast-food entrances. In each of these scenes, students should identify the sort of place the scene is, the types of activities that take place there, the people who engage in those activities, and the shared objectives of those people. Overall, students should seek to answer these questions: In what ways do people in these scenes use the genre—and what are the reasons or purposes for the genre? It might be necessary for teachers to encourage students to go beyond the obvious; in my example, the obvious purpose of the genre is to sell and/or buy a used car. However, there are other purposes for people who use this genre: to save money or recoup it, to eliminate unnecessary expenses, to do a favor for a relative. Students need to think beyond the surface.

■ Next, have students investigate the situation within the scene. To simplify the want ad example for class instruction, for instance, I might examine only one situation within the broader scene—the situation of a newspaper want ad to sell a car. Within that situation, students should determine, as much as possible, the interactions of the participants and the roles each is expected to play. So, for example, the person who places the ad has something she expects someone else wants, while the person responding to the ad is in need of something another has. This creates an unequal relationship in some regards—unless the seller is desperate and the buyer is "just looking." In that case, the relationship shifts. Determining motives and relationships from the ads alone, however, may be difficult. But students should consider that those who would look for cars in newspaper want ad sections might be different customers than those who would look online or at postings on a grocery store's bulletin board. As you explore one situation, help students realize how the other situations would possibly engender different characteristics. For instance, someone reading the booklet while he eats at the fast-food restaurant may simply be passing the time, interested but not really ready to buy—a fairly unengaged participant in the scene. Students' explorations of these situations and the spaces they make for participants to act in should help them understand the nature of genres more thoroughly.

■ Next, have students examine and analyze several examples of the genre. If a genre is short, students can examine a larger number (an encouragement to select a short genre for this exploration), such as all of the used car ads in the Sunday newspaper. Have them look for patterns of features and consider the following aspects suggested by Devitt, Reiff, and Bawarshi:

- Content: What ideas does this genre include? What does it leave out?
- Structure: How are the ideas organized in the genre? How does the organization privilege certain ideas over others?
- Format: How is the genre formatted? What visual elements (font size and white space, for example) seem to be expected?
- Language: What kind of language is used? What level of formality is found in word choice? What tone is used?
- Sentences: What kinds of sentences are usual? Short or long? Direct or winding? (94)

If students have a wide range of samples to explore, they should notice variety in most of these areas, although some more structured genres have less flexibility in what they allow. However, most genres allow for some variety, and students should see this.

■ After students have a good understanding of the genre, have them connect the patterns they found with the situation(s) the genre responds to. To do this, students should think of why the patterns they observed exist in this genre. Have them use questions like the following to come to conclusions about how genres work in specific situations:

- What roles do the patterns suggest for participants?
- What attitudes are represented by the patterns of the genre?
- What actions do the patterns allow and constrain?
- What values are represented by the genre and its patterns?

By considering these questions and thus connecting patterns in the texts to the participants and situations, students become more aware of how genres function in social settings—and become more aware of aspects of genres, such as their variability and contextual nature. From this awareness, students become more sensitive to the ways genres act in their lives and the ways they act with genres.

Devitt suggests that teachers begin teaching genre awareness to young students with language explorations that help them see "how language differs in different situations and how those differences relate to different purposes" (*Writing* 198). Gregory Shafer explains how he used letters to different audiences to help his (mostly immigrant) students gain the beginning of genre awareness. As his students wrote letters to friends and to potential employers, they discussed the implications of language choice and how it was connected to power relationships between the writer and the reader of the letters. Although Shafer never mentions genre theory, his lessons develop genre awareness in his students as they gain a sense of how good writing adapts to situation—considering purposes and audiences, settings and relationships.

UNDERSTANDING GENRE AS READER EXPECTATION

Genres don't only give ideas of how to act in certain situations; they also give us clues as to how to read certain situations. Bomer's example of a program handed to him in a theater, described in Chapter 1, shows how situation is inherent to genre. But Freadman notes that the relation of formal properties of text with context "does not mean . . . that the formal properties of a genre cannot travel" ("Anyone" in Reid 117). Genres can be, and often are, engaged for purposes beyond those intended in their original situation. This flexibility inherent in genre is an important concept for students to understand as they develop as writers: it means they have choices as writers, but it also means they have responsibilities to readers and to situations.

Students can begin to understand how genre establishes reader expectation by examining the book *Dragonology: The Complete Book of Dragons* by Dugald A. Steer (writing as Ernest Drake). By questioning the genres used to present the fake facts in *Dragonology*—charts, graphs, timelines, etc—students can appreciate how genres carry expectations (of truthfulness? of factuality? of pretense?) beyond the content of each piece. They can see that we approach genres with reader expectations because past experiences and current situations prepare us to do so. Therefore, writers know that they can count on readers to have a beginning stance toward their texts because of genre. To help students understand this aspect of genre, I use a book by Robert N. Munsch, *The Paper Bag Princess*.

■ Ask students to look at the cover and the title and anticipate what kind of a story this will be. "A fairy tale!" is always the answer I get because the cover shows a picture of a dragon and the title names a princess . . . so students use the frame of reference they have that puts the two together.

■ Then, ask them to name the characteristics they expect as readers of a fairy tale. As they state their expectations, list them on the board. Usually I get at least the following: a handsome prince; magic; some problem that has to be overcome, usually by magic; a castle; a prince who saves the princess; love; a happily-ever-after ending.

■ Next, read the story to the students. Tell them to watch for the ways the story meets their expectations and ways it doesn't. As the story starts, it seems that it will be what they expect, but very quickly students see Elizabeth, the princess, confronting the dragon to save the prince. And she manages to thwart the dragon through brains rather than brawn. The ending, though, is the most surprising: when Prince Ronald fails to appreciate Elizabeth's actions to rescue him because he objects to her appearance, she responds: "Ronald, your clothes are really pretty and your hair is very neat. You look like a real prince, but you are a bum." The two don't get married, reversing the expected ending for a fairy tale.

■ After you've finished reading the story—and the students have had their chuckle over the ending—ask them to identify ways the story meets their expectations of a fairy tale. My students usually note that it has a prince, a princess, a dragon, a castle, magic, and a problem. Then, ask how it does not meet their expectations. Obviously: the ending, but also the role reversal (the princess saving the prince) and the brain/brawn reversal. Ask them if it is still a fairy tale. I've never had students say that it isn't, so I ask: Why is it still a fairy tale if it doesn't meet all your expectations? Students quickly come to see that the genre has flexibility, that enough aspects of their expectations have been met so as to satisfy them that what they expected was what they got. The little twists are creative, not genre breaking.

■ Next, ask them to speculate how far a writer could twist a fairy tale until it is no longer a fairy tale. At what point would we feel misled—thinking we were getting one thing but getting another? This is interesting for students to consider. They often find that the boundaries are very flexible, but twisting enough of them gives them a new genre, a fable or a fantasy or something else. At this point it can be helpful to bring in some other stories that stretch the boundaries of readers' expectations and test their conclusions. *An Undone Fairy Tale* by Ian Lendler is one possibility. In that book, the author and illustrator interrupt the story to talk to the reader, giving instructions about how to read the story. The result is comical. Is it still a fairy tale or is the author using readers' expectations of a fairy tale to do something else?

■ Finally, ask students to consider how they might read *The Paper Bag Princess* if they didn't have any exposure to fairy tales and, therefore, no reader expectations for the genre. What would be different? Most students are able to see that the humor of the story, the ending, and some of the twists that add interest for them as readers would not be as meaningful without the established expectations.

■ It is important at this point to discuss how genre knowledge can affect all our reading: if we pick up a text and don't know what to expect from it, will we understand it in the same way that readers who are familiar with the context and the genre do? Will we know the "road signs" to look for to make the most effective meaning of the text? I tell students of the first time I've read certain documents—my first teaching contract, directions for applying for a rebate, tenure files—and how in each case the reading challenged me initially because I had to make sense of the genre first: what its role was in the situation, who wrote it, what that person wanted to accomplish, what my role was as a reader, and what aspects of the text mattered most for the purpose and situation.

■ Cooper writes that "knowledge of genres is essential to reading and writing, making reading comprehensible and writing possible" (25). Is this statement true or not? How do reading strategies differ when we know a genre and when we do not? Have students write responses to this quote and these questions and discuss them to refine their understanding of the role of genre in their own reading experience.

■ In *Scenes of Writing: Strategies for Composing with Genres*, the authors include an activity that relates to the concept of this lesson. They ask students to "list at least 10 different genres you read, including if possible at least one genre that you read on a computer. Remember to include not just formal or school genres, and not just literary genres but also the everyday genres you read, like the backs of cereal boxes. Then pick three of these genres and write a paragraph describing how differently you read each of them" (Devitt, Reiff, and Bawarshi 50).

Have students complete this activity to individualize the idea of reading with genre knowledge and to reflect on how they already use such knowledge in their own reading lives. The reflection should help them consider even further how they can apply genre knowledge to future reading experiences.

BLURRING GENRE BOUNDARIES

To see that genres have flexibility, students can explore a variety of examples of a genre they already know to discover the range that a genre can take. One genre that I have found interesting for this exploration is what I call how-to writing and others sometimes call process writing. Most students are familiar with this kind of writing, and an abundance of examples is available. Teachers can follow the ideas of this application with a number of genres, as long as a wide assortment of examples is available. (A slightly different version of this application is found in my book *Strategic Writing: The Writing Process and Beyond in the Secondary English Classroom*.)

■ Begin by collecting samples of how-to writing: furniture or bicycle assembly instructions, game instructions, directions to get from one place to another—or try mining www.ehow.com for directions on just about everything. I also include humorous versions of how-to writing that show the blurring of boundaries. Online I found "Cat Bathing as a Martial Art" by Howard "Bud" Herron (available at http://www.tlcpoodles.com/catbath.html). I also use "Slice of Life" by Russell Baker, a humorous commentary on slicing a turkey written in a how-to format. Finally, I try to make sure I have some versions of how-to writing that use the form to describe what *not* to do. A simple version is *How to Lose All Your Friends* by Nancy Carlson, but another is "How to Write a Really Bad Essay" by J. Gladman (available at http://www.durham.edu. on.ca/grassroots/oxfordtutor/badessay.html). Some satirical examples of how-to writing include William Safire's "How to Read a Column" (a challenging example for students to grasp but important to show how context matters). Another example, and one that also moves into the realm of social commentary is "Game Ball: How to Shamelessly Use Your Child to Get an Autographed Baseball" by Frank Lalli.

■ With a wide variety of examples at hand, begin by asking students what they know about the context for how-to writing (or whatever type of writing you're showing). Who writes these texts? Who reads them? Why? In what context and situation do they expect to find this kind of writing? Why?

- After they've discussed the context, have students generate a list of characteristics for the genre. For each characteristic, ask them to consider why that characteristic would be expected for the purpose and context of the genre. At this point, it is important to have students explore the more traditional examples you've collected. Students can generate more ideas and see if their expectations for the genre are confirmed.

- The next step is valuable for students to begin to see the blurring of boundaries. Let them examine the less traditional examples and find ways that those examples meet the expectations and ways they don't. As students examine the samples used for other purposes (humor or social commentary), discuss their contexts. Are they the same? Are the pieces of writing really trying to do the same thing—or are they doing something else? What students may find is that using the expectations for one purpose and context in another context and for alternate purposes blurs the lines of genre as a social response. Aspects of the form stay much the same: in how-to writing, these formal aspects might include the use of imperatives, the numbered list, the explanations that elaborate the directions. But the content shifts to accommodate the new purpose/situation. Language shifts to create a different tone, a different relationship between the reader and the writer. Ask students to consider and discuss why the characteristics of one genre can accomplish other purposes in other contexts.

- Next, ask students to consider other examples they know of genre boundaries being blurred, of genres being used in ways other than in the contexts and for the purposes they originally were designed. For examples, students might look at memoirs or novels that are written as a series of poems (*Learning to Swim: A Memoir* by Ann Turner, *Make Lemonade* by Virginia Euwer Wolff, *Out of the Dust* and *Witness* by Karen Hesse) and explore why authors would choose to blur the boundaries that way. Are the books poems or novels? Older students might find it interesting to consider nonfiction books that read more like novels: *Seabiscuit* by Laura Hillenbrand and *The Devil in the White City: Murder, Magic, and Madness at the Fair That Changed America* by Erik Larson, for example. Again, why the blurring of boundaries? What does that tell us about the genres? About contexts? About purposes? Kress says: "I expect genres to occur in a certain *place,* and when they appear out of their place I wonder what is going on. 'Lifting' a genre from one context and putting it in another . . . is an innovative act, an act of creativity. It changes not just the genre, not just my relation to the text, but the new context in which it occurs" ("Genre and the Changing" 467). Have students discuss Kress's statement and their experiences with blurring or lifted genres.

■ Finally, have students reflect on the ways blurred boundaries can be acts of creativity, of rebellion even. Devitt comments on the increased use of personal letters that are really sales pitches. "Such attempts to use form to mislead us about the actual genre again indicate the separability of formal features from the essence of a genre" (*Writing* 12). Have students think about the manipulative aspects of blurred boundaries. In reflections, have them consider possible positive and negative consequences to using blurred genre boundaries in their own lives.

5 Teaching about Genres

LEARNING UNFAMILIAR GENRES

Some theorists believe students can learn strategies for acquiring genres by practicing them in a classroom setting. Although I acknowledge the importance of genre acquisition by immersion in a context, I agree with Devitt, who argues that such acquisition suggests students have a prior understanding of the kinds of things to be aware of when encountering new genres: "Further instruction in how to learn new genres might aid their learning" (*Writing* 195). Such instruction, however, depends on its effectiveness, including the "richness of discursive context" (Freedman, "Situating" 188) and a thorough understanding of genre theory. In fact, Hicks, in her study of genre learning in an elementary classroom, found support for John Dixon's claim that the "social dialogue, rather than texts as formal and grammatical structures" (474), promoted genre learning, and this supports theorists' assertions about the importance of the classroom as a context for learning.

The following application provides strategies not necessarily for performing a genre (although that is one outcome some teachers attempt); rather the strategies are more for practicing how to learn new genres when confronted with them. As Devitt asserts, "teaching for genre awareness may appear similar in some respects to teaching for genre acquisition, but the ends make all the difference" (*Writing* 198). I would add that a teacher's understanding of genres would be important also. If a teacher, after working through the application, asks students to write an imitation of the genres they've explored, that teacher would understand the limitations of such work in the context of the classroom—and not expect that the actions of the genre, the essence of it, would be carried out. The students would simply be showing their understanding of the ideas, presentation, and represented roles of a genre—not the actual genre itself. This application relies on suggestions from Sarah Andrew-Vaughan and Cathy Fleischer. As they describe in their article, student performance of the genre is only a small portion of the grade; the real work of the project is the research into the genre itself, an idea that reflects contemporary genre theory.

   ▪ Begin by having students select an unfamiliar genre. It could be one that they anticipate using in the near future (a job application or a college application essay, for example), although it could also be any genre they are unfamiliar with but would like to know more about (song lyrics or Web page). Andrew-Vaughan and Fleischer provide lists of possible genres for their students, but the trick is to make sure students actually choose an unfamiliar genre. When they've each chosen one, have them write a letter explaining their choice to you.

■ Next, have students consider the situations in which the selected genre is performed. If they find it used in a variety of situations, have them limit their selection to a particular situation and then write about that one:

- Where is the genre used?
- What is the interaction it accomplishes?
- Who uses the genre and to do what?
- What subjects does the genre discuss?
- What relationships does the genre suggest?
- What roles does the genre suggest for participants?

■ After the exploration of context, have students collect assorted samples of the unfamiliar genre. They need as many as they can get, but a minimum of five is my recommendation. If the samples are too similar, they would need to collect more. Have them examine the samples to find common patterns and variations—not just in format or obvious features, but also in ideas, in language, in ideologies, and in the relationships created by the genre. Have them consider if the genre relates to other genres, including if it responds to another genre or instigates a response genre. All their questions and guesses should be recorded in notes (or research journals, as suggested by Andrew-Vaughan and Fleischer) each time they work on the project; whichever you or your students choose, notes or a journal, should serve as a record and reflection of the questions students explore and the answers they discover. Working through this process as a class with a single text first can help students who don't have experience in looking so deeply into a genre. If this project is conducted as a workshop, the teacher can help students through the individual questioning process.

■ When students have explored the genre thoroughly, have them show their understanding of it in different ways. The goal of this application isn't necessarily the production of a text that looks like the unfamiliar genre students have researched. Instead, as Devitt notes, the purposes of building genre awareness "are for students to understand the intricate connections between contexts and forms, to perceive potential ideological effects of genres, and to discern both constraints and choices that genres make possible" (*Writing* 198). Teachers can evaluate students' journals or notes to see if such goals were achieved. However, students can also attempt to imitate the genre (and some want to after their explorations), or they could simply write up their conclusions about the genre as a final reflective piece to accompany the investigation journal they kept. Irene Clark suggests writing an analysis paper, with the "thesis . . . a claim about what a particular genre tells us about how people respond to and experience a particular situation" ("Genre" 244). That analysis paper would also reflect genre understanding.

CRITIQUING FAMILIAR GENRES

While implementing the genre awareness approach advocated by Devitt, Reiff, and Bawarshi in *Scenes of Writing,* Bastian found that students did not adequately critique familiar genres. In investigating this response, she found published evidence (Adrian Clynes and Alex Henry) that her students were not unique: students in a variety of situations found only single purposes for familiar genres. Bastian calls this the *genre effect* and argues for having students question familiar genres in ways that will expand their concept of genre.

Beyond helping them expand their understanding of genre theory, such critiquing can also help students develop their ability to act with genres by allowing them to see the possibilities inherent in them. As Devitt, Reiff, and Bawarshi assert, "Writers cannot resist or modify conventions unless they know what these conventions are and what they do. . . . Writers are not creative by accident, nor do they make creative choices simply for the heck of it. Very often, their choices are informed and purposeful. They have a reason for making the choices that they do, and what is more, they know which patterns within the genre they can modify and which ones they had better not. This knowledge is important since, if writers modify too many essential elements of the genre at once, the audience will no longer be able to recognize the genre at all, defeating the purpose" (149). Critiquing a genre, questioning what it does and how it does it as well as what values and attitudes it represents, can enhance students' abilities to use genres to accomplish their own purposes.

Furthermore, such critical thinking about genres enables students to understand more fully the ways genres are used and appropriated in the world around them. In *Scenes of Writing,* Devitt, Reiff, and Bawarshi refer to sweepstakes companies who use official-looking documents or letters to suggest the legitimacy of their claims: "Banking on the fact that we will be fooled by the legal-sounding language, such companies try to convince us to take their offers seriously" (152). Alfie Kohn counted on our expectations of a genre when he created the "advertisement" found in the *English Journal* issue on assessment (Figure 2). In his "ad," genre expectations contribute to our understanding of the piece as satire. Learning how to critique genres will prepare students to deal with the ways some people use genre expectations to mislead others—and help them understand when genres are being used to carry other messages as well. As Devitt, Reiff, and Bawarshi note, "some genres privilege the needs of some users over the needs of other users. . . . Genres may limit other possible values and beliefs. . . . People misinterpret or misuse these generic strategies. . . . Genres do not always operate smoothly or effectively within their scenes of writing. They do not always communicate what we intend or expect them to, or we may not want to communicate what genres encourage us to" (152). If students can critique the genres in use around them, in addition to understanding the way genres may be employed to influence them, they will more likely be able to understand why some genres they use may fail to accomplish what they hoped they would.

■ Begin questioning a genre by examining it as a whole class. I have used the disclosure document that sets up the rules and procedures of the classroom for this whole-class examination. Use some of the questions listed later in this lesson to encourage students to consider what the genre does and how it does it, who it privileges, and how the tone, language, and format contribute to that privileging.

■ Following this discussion, ask students, either individually or in small groups, to rewrite all or part of the genre, changing the ideas, the format, the voice, or the language so that the relationships and situation are somewhat altered. When they have done so, discuss the changes and have students consider what those changes did to the genre: How is it different? Would it still function as it is supposed to? Why or why not? How are participants' roles changed by the revisions? Once a mother called me in the morning before classes started, worried that her daughter would be penalized for the tone she used in rewriting a section of our disclosure document. The girl's revision was something like this: *Your butt had better be on the seat when the first tone of the bell sounds. If one cheek is hanging off, too bad for you. You will still be marked tardy and penalized.* Certainly the tone and diction had changed the genre—the relationship between teacher and student and, therefore, the situation—but the girl understood completely what she had done and what it had done to the action of the genre. That's what I wanted.

Accelerated Direct Success
Because Test Scores Matter More Than Learning

At **ADS**, we believe your school should be doing whatever is necessary to improve results on standardized tests. Fortunately (if you can afford us), we're here to help—with techniques based on scientific research.*

Worried about subjecting students to endless worksheets? Don't be. Our worksheets have been computerized, with bells and whistles added to disguise their reliance on mind-numbing rote instruction. In no time, you'll hear children chanting phonemes in unison and memorizing math facts on command . . . so you can be sure they're on their way to becoming enthusiastic lifelong learners.

On the basis of higher scores on a single low-level, multiple-choice, norm-referenced test, **ADS** has already been selected as a "research-validated program" by the U.S. Department of Education, New American Schools, and the American Federation of Teachers!

* Driller et al., "Reinforcement Parameters in Rattus norvegicus," Journal of Behaviorist Dogma 71 (1990): 516-89.

With **ADS**, you get minute-by-minute teaching guides, thousands of practice tests, and other materials for turning your school into a 21st-century test-preparation factory. Unlike its competitors, **ADS** also sends you specially designed pellet dispensers that fit on each student's desk and shoot candy directly into the child's mouth when he or she emits a correct answer. Best of all, the same apparatus delivers a mild electric shock to any student who asks a question unrelated to your state's standards. (But don't worry! They learn quickly to stop asking!)

The **ADS** Platinum Edition also comes with a powerful new super-adhesive so you can have students glued to their seats during lectures. Literally.

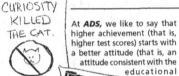

At **ADS**, we like to say that higher achievement (that is, higher test scores) starts with a better attitude (that is, an attitude consistent with the educational doctrine approved by your state's top policy makers and corporate executives). And what better way to "set the mood" than with a series of colorful posters for your classroom walls, featuring such slogans as:

- Curiosity Killed the Cat
- Ours Is Not to Reason Why—Ours Is Just to Multiply
- Fonnix Worked for Me
- Sir! More worksheets, please, sir!

"By following the ADS idiotproof Curriculum™, I no longer have to waste time worrying about how to create assignments or assessments. In fact, I no longer have to worry about students at all. Thank you, ADS!"

—4th grade teacher

"ADS raised our school's scores on the Isolated Skills Test by nearly 3%—and all we had to do was eliminate science and the arts."

—Principal

Simply select our convenient direct-billing option, and we'll make the arrangements so that **ADS, Inc.** automatically receives all the funds in your budget that you probably would have just spent on "staff development" or "books."

Then tell your teachers and students to leave the thinking to us!

For more information, visit our website:
www.drilltodeath.com

Figure 2. Genre Expectations in Play

■ Next, have students consider the discourse communities to which they belong. Peagler and Yancey suggest having students "create two representations . . . a verbal explanation and a visual map" (156–57). Some students like the idea of a list, but others like the idea of a chart and think it helps them see their relationships and communities better. Either way, help students find ways to identify all the discourse communities they belong to. They can start with groups like friends, family, church, and school. They might also have work groups they interact with. Within each of the broader areas—or as separate communities—students might have teams or clubs or other smaller groups. Exploring these different communities and considering how they use language differently among them—the kinds of things they talk about, the language and documents they use to communicate, the kinds of relationships they have—can help students understand more about how genres work differently, even when they might look somewhat alike at first glance.

■ Then, have students look within one of these communities and find a familiar genre they interact with. (Short ones are better, since then the activities that follow won't be so lengthy.) When they have chosen a genre, have students analyze it, seeing what it does and how it does it for the specific community from which they have drawn it, following the whole-class example described previously. As part of this analysis, they could use the following questions suggested in *Scenes for Writing* for critiquing genres:

- What does the genre allow its users to do and what does it not allow them to do?
- Whose needs are most served by the genre? Whose needs are least served? . . .
- Does the genre enable its users to represent themselves fully? . . .
- Does the genre create inequalities among its users that lead to imbalances of power?
- Do the assumptions that the genre reflects privilege certain ways of doing things? . . .
- Does the genre allow its users to do certain things at the expense of others? And if so, at what cost? (Devitt, Reiff, and Bawarshi 161)

These questions can help students come to understand more fully the contexts in which they perform familiar genres. This needs to be done in consideration, though, of Devitt's assertion, which I support, that "no one could ever fully describe all the contextualized features of any genre. Even experts in a genre . . . cannot fully articulate either the necessary features of nor reasons behind a specific genre they often use" (*Writing* 194). The point of the questioning is to increase understanding of some concepts about genres (particularly their ideologies) more than it is to construct thoroughly every aspect of a genre's influence.

- After they've analyzed the genre, have them change it. I suggest giving them options, since sometimes they have trouble visualizing how a genre can be changed (the genre effect, again). Some options include these: the formality of the language, the diction (from slang to professional, for example), the kind of ideas addressed, the order of ideas, or the format used. Students can use one or more of these suggestions.

- When they've rewritten the genre, have students write a reflection about what they changed, why they changed it, and what difference it makes to the genre—to how it is or could be used, as well as to the changes it would make in the relationships normally enacted through the genre.

- As part of this questioning, add an exploration of how writers use familiar genres for alternate purposes. Because genres privilege ways of seeing and establish roles for participants, writers take advantage of that and use those inherent expectations for their own ends. One example is found at http://www.coxar.pwp.blueyonder.co.uk/. This page looks like an error screen but is actually a political commentary about weapons of mass destruction. Teachers can find other examples in Dave Barry's writing; he often makes use of genres (such as plays) for commentary rather than entertainment. Students can search out examples in popular culture—on television (using what appears to be a newscast to promote a product or provide commentary on news) or in magazines. More and more often, companies are putting video skits online that they hope will sell their products. If the skit is successful, it gets passed around the Internet, much like other entertaining videos. The companies use the entertainment factor as a way to advertise—for a lot less money. These "ads" are more subtle; they use one genre (entertaining video skits) to really accomplish another purpose: advertising. In so doing, they alter relationships from those regularly enacted by traditional advertising. For one thing, viewers seek them out instead of muting them. Discussing how familiar genres are used in alternate ways can expand students' understanding of genre beyond its form or expected use.

COMPARING GENRE STRATEGIES

Sometimes as teachers we tell students there are four (or five or some other number of) ways to begin a paper for school: a question, a startling fact, a quotation, an anecdote . . . By doing so, we think we give students strategies, but students often use those suggestions as formulas. Not every kind of writing should use one of those options as an introductory technique. Not even every research paper or analysis essay should. By implying that there is a limited number of ways to begin any piece of writing, we remove the rhetorical aspect—the strategic aspect—from writing. We suggest that writing is fill-in-the-blank or even multiple choice when it is really much more open-ended than that. Genres have constraints, yes, but they also have flexibility. And because of creativity and innovation, writers can (and do) use even basic strategies in ways no one has before.

Comprone sees value in approaching genre learning from a strategic perspective: "If genres are best conceived of as discourse strategies, then we as teachers must provide opportunities for students to use them as strategies as they compose" (105). Performing with genres means being strategic and rhetorical—considering purpose and situation but also considering options to address our purposes in varying situations. The following application explains one way to show students how they can consider genre strategies for introductions and conclusions in research-based writing, approaches beyond the traditional ones suggested by quick lists of methods. I suggest using this application during the drafting or revising processes when students are writing a research-based paper. A similar process can be used with other aspects of many genres as long as the approach is strategic, not formulaic.

- Begin by asking students about the strategic purposes for introductions in this genre. How are they different from introductions in other genres they know? Since the context is school writing, students may not see a difference between this kind of writing—a type of show-what-you've-learned-from-research writing—and other genres unique to school. Encourage them to seek out dissimilarities in situations and purposes.

- Provide students with many examples of the aspect of the genre under consideration. For this application, I show students several introductions from informative writing, and I've included some of those here. Put them on overhead transparencies to make class discussion possible. After reading them, discuss what the various writers did to begin. Ask these questions (or ones like them) to help students see these options as strategic and also connected to genre and context.

- What did the writer do? What strategy did he/she employ?
- Why might that be an effective choice or strategy to do the job of introducing this kind of writing?
- What kind of relationship between reader and writer does the introduction suggest? How is it appropriate to the genre?
- How does the introduction suggest a position for the reader to take? How did the author create that suggestion for the reader?

From Bill Bryson's *A Short History of Nearly Everything:*

> Welcome. And congratulations. I am delighted that you could make it. Getting here wasn't easy. I know. In fact, I suspect it was a little tougher than you realize.
> To begin with, for you to be here now trillions of drifting atoms had somehow to assemble in an intricate and intriguingly obliging manner to create you. It's an arrangement so specialized and particular that it has never been tried before and will only exist this once. . . . Why atoms take this trouble is a bit of a puzzle. Being you is not a gratifying experience at the atomic level. (1)

From Hillenbrand's *Seabiscuit: An American Legend:*

> In 1938, near the end of a decade of monumental turmoil, the year's number one newsmaker was not Franklin Delano Roosevelt, Hitler, or Mussolini. It wasn't Pope Pius XI, nor was it Lou Gehrig, Howard Hughes, or Clark Gable. The subject of the most newspaper column inches in 1938 wasn't even a person. It was an undersized, crooked-legged racehorse named Seabiscuit. (xix)

From Mark Kurlansky's *Salt: A World History:*

> I bought the rock in Spanish Catalonia, in the rundown hillside mining town of Cardona. An irregular pink trapezoid with elongated, curved indentations etched on its surface by raindrops, it had an odd translucence and appeared to be a cross between rose quartz and soap. The resemblance to soap came from the fact that it dissolved in water and its edges were worn smooth like a used soap bar. (1)

From Bruce Feiler's *Walking the Bible: A Journey by Land through the Five Books of Moses:*

> The call to prayer sounded just after 3 P.M. It came from a minaret, echoed off the storefronts, and stopped me, briefly, in the middle of the street. All around, people halted their hurrying and turned their attention, momentarily, to God. A few old men pulled cloaks around their shoulders and slipped into the back of a shop. Two

boys rushed across the road and disappeared behind a stone wall. A woman picked up her basket of radishes and tiptoed out of sight. Part of me felt odd to be starting a journey into the roots of the Bible in a place so spiritually removed from my own. But continuing toward the center of town, I realized my unease might be a reminder of a truth tucked away in the early verses of Genesis: Abraham was not originally the man he became. He was not an Israelite, he was not a Jew. He was not even a believer in God—at least initially. He was a traveler, called by some voice not entirely clear that said: Go, head to this land, walk along this route, and trust what you will find. (3)

From Simon Winchester's *The Professor and the Madman: A Tale of Murder, Insanity and the Making of the* Oxford English Dictionary:

Popular myth has it that one of the most remarkable conversations in modern history took place on a cool and misty late autumn afternoon in 1896, in the small village of Crowthorne in the county of Berkshire.

One of the parties to the colloquy was the formidable Dr. James Murray, the editor of the *Oxford English Dictionary*. On the day in question, he traveled fifty miles by train from Oxford to meet an enigmatic figure named Dr. W. C. Minor, who was among the most prolific of the thousands of volunteer contributors whose labors lay at the core of the dictionary's creation. (xi)

▪ After using the questions to explore the possibilities for introducing research-based writing like the examples here, have students consider their own writing. What does it have in common with the samples that would allow some strategies used in them to be effective? What roles for reader and writer does the students' situation establish that are similar to those in the examples? How could the ideas, the language, or the stance of the samples be adapted strategically for their own writing? After they consider the questions, have them practice two or more of the strategies and work with partners to see which is more effective for their particular situations. In this way, they should begin to see the options presented across the samples as just that—options that can be considered but can't be adopted wholesale without taking into account their own situations for writing.

▪ When students are ready to write conclusions, ask them to discuss the strategic value of conclusions for research-based writing. What purposes does a conclusion serve and how does it accomplish these?

▪ When examining conclusions, it's harder to discern strategies from the examples because the conclusions are harder to understand without the content before them. I try to choose conclusions that can stand alone but still show options. Follow the same process and questioning with the sample conclusions as was practiced with the introductions.

From Bryson's *A Short History of Nearly Everything:*

> If this book has a lesson, it is that we are awfully lucky to be here—and by "we" I mean every living thing. To attain any kind of life in this universe of ours appears to be quite an achievement. As humans we are doubly lucky, of course: We enjoy not only the privilege of existence but also the singular ability to appreciate it and even, in a multitude of ways, to make it better. It is a talent we have only barely begun to grasp.
>
> We have arrived at this position of eminence in a stunningly short time. Behaviorally modern human beings—that is, people who can speak and make art and organize complex activities—have existed for only about 0.0001 percent of Earth's history. But surviving for even that little while has required a nearly endless string of good fortune.
>
> We really are at the beginning of it all. The trick, of course, is to make sure we never find the end. And that, almost certainly, will require a good deal more than lucky breaks. (478)

From Kurlansky's *Salt: A World History:*

> In the past, this kind of fine, white salt was called in Celtic *holen gwenn,* white salt, and was rare and expensive, only for the best tables and the finest salted foods. The gray was the cheap everyday salt. The relative value of the white and gray salt is a question of supply, demand, and labor, but also culture, history, and the fashion of the times.
>
> Why should salt that is washed be cheaper than salt with dirt? Fixing the true value of salt, one of earth's most accessible commodities, has never been easy. (449)

From Eric Schlosser's *Fast Food Nation: The Dark Side of the All-American Meal:*

> Pull open the glass door, feel the rush of cool air, walk inside, get in line, and look around you, look at the kids working in the kitchen, at the customers in their seats, at the ads for the latest toys, study the backlit color photographs above the counter, think about where the food came from, about how and where it was made, about what is set in motion by every single fast food purchase, the ripple effect near and far, think about it. Then place your order. Or turn and walk out the door. It's not too late. Even in this fast food nation, you can still have it your way. (269–70)

From Jane Yolen and Heidi Elisabet Yolen Stemple's *The Wolf Girls: An Unsolved Mystery from History* (this nonfiction picture book has a different type of ending, but it can be adapted for some topics that don't have tidy conclusions):

> So what really happened?
> No one knows for sure.
> But now that you have read the story and looked at my notes and word lists, maybe you can solve the mystery of the wolf girls. Maybe one of the stories about how they were discovered seems right to you. Or maybe you'll come up with a theory of your own.
> Just remember, as my dad always says: Check Your Clues. [A summary of the four current theories follows.]

▪ As with the introductions, have students consider and discuss the conclusion strategies used in these examples. How do they accomplish the purposes of conclusions in research-based writing? How do they reinforce participant roles? Which strategies would best fit the situation of their individual papers? Have students practice some strategies and then work with others to select what best accomplishes their purposes, so as to reinforce their understanding that writing is both individual and social.

SEEING GENRES AS DYNAMIC

Especially since students see the genres taught in schools (five-paragraph essays, book reports, research papers) as unchanging, it is important for them to comprehend that genres do change over time—and that people and situations influence those changes. This lesson helps students examine genres as they transform through time to meet different purposes and also see how a writer can use readers' genre expectations to carry messages beyond those originally intended, thus teaching the flexibility of genres.

▪ Ask students to share what they know about wanted posters: What do they look like? What purpose(s) do they serve? In what situations are they found? Who uses them? List their responses on the board.

▪ As a class, review several examples of wanted posters from the Old West and from more current times found on websites. Some possibilities are listed here:

- This is a good site for Old West wanted posters: http://www.wild westweb.net/reward.html.
- This site has a few wanted posters from the Old West: http://www.tombstone1880.com/wildbill/wanted.htm.

– This site shows a number of traditional wanted posters from the early 1900s: http://libweb.princeton.edu/libraries/firestone/rbsc/aids/WC127/.

– This website has modern wanted posters: http://www.fbi.gov/wanted.htm.

After they've examined examples of wanted posters, have students note aspects they didn't list on the board and confirm what they already noticed. Be sure to have students pay attention to the variety among the examples and the ways the different aspects of the posters fulfill different purposes. As students note each particular feature, ask why that feature is important to the overall (or to a specific) purpose of wanted posters. For example, why include the amount of the reward or the crime for which the person is wanted? Connecting textual features to purpose, even if they're speculating, is important for students in considering genre.

▪ Using examples from websites (or other sources), students should work in small groups to fill out Venn diagrams comparing and contrasting Old West wanted posters with modern ones. Have them discuss what they discover.

▪ When students have completed their exploration and discussion, review their findings and relate what they found to the purpose of the genre. Connect the differences to the particular situations and times. For example, many Old West posters don't include a picture of the wanted person. Perhaps the outlaw was well known in an area, so an image was unnecessary. The availability of photographs might also contribute to this aspect of the genre that we now consider essential. This short comparison should help students see that genres (even one considered as formulaic as this one is) have variety, change over time, and adapt to specific purposes and situations.

▪ As a follow-up, have students (individually or in small groups) find examples of other genres that have been used for more than fifty years. They might consider ads in newspapers or magazines, news articles, wedding announcements, diaries, letters, even poems or children's picture books. Have them work through this same process with their examples, questioning context first and then looking at the changes through time. Make sure they connect the changes they see to situation and purpose. Then have them present their findings to the class so that other students can see that some genres have changed more than others in about the same amount of time. From their investigation, have students draw conclusions about what causes genres to transform and why some change less than others. (The five-paragraph essay, for example, has been modified very little, if at all, in fifty years.)

- Finally, have students reflect on their own purposes for using genres and how these might contribute, if only incrementally, to genre change—or consider when they might need to be more instrumental in altering a genre.

DESTABILIZING RIGID GENRE CONCEPTIONS

Because as Johns notes, "our curricular tendencies are to emphasize regularities and to search for stability so that students can learn some concrete facts about texts," teachers sometimes have a tendency to reduce school genres to rigid formulas ("Destabilizing" 238). The five-paragraph essay is an example of that tendency. As an antecedent genre, Devitt sees some value to it: "The five-paragraph theme provides a sense of organization and thesis that can adapt to organic structures and controlling ideas" (*Writing* 207). But that benefit will be of value only if, as Coe asserts, students learn that "there is an important distinction between mastering a genre and being mastered by it" ("New Rhetoric" 198). With inadequate theories of genre, students won't be able to adapt the school structures they've learned because they won't see the difference Coe addresses. As Johns argues, "one of the issues about which genre theorists and pedagogues should be more concerned . . . is the nature of the genre theories that our students bring with them to class. Some of these theories, particularly the rich, complete ones about the 'homely' genres of their own families and cultures, can assist them to apply social constructionist views to academic and professional genres. . . . However, other theories, such as the limited ones they may have acquired in school, need to be destabilized, enriched, and expanded" ("Destabilizing" 246).

One way to destabilize rigid genre conceptions is to teach what Devitt refers to as "nontraditional academic genres, like literacy narratives or ethnographies" because, she asserts, doing so "creates antecedent genres for students that will also change how they potentially approach new writing tasks" (*Writing* 206). Students can and do borrow from antecedent genres when writing, giving them new ways to approach those situations that seem to call for rigid forms. Another way to destabilize rigid genre conceptions is described in the application that follows. It is best used when students have written a five-paragraph essay they can use for the lesson.

■ Have students review what they know about five-paragraph essays. Extend their understanding beyond the form by discussing the following questions:

- What is a good situation in which to use the five-paragraph essay?
- When might it be an inappropriate or a poor choice?
- What are the beliefs and values suggested by the five-paragraph essay form?
- What are the roles the form assigns to writers and readers?

Help students to understand that, like other genres, there is more to the five-paragraph essay than the form: it carries ideologies, and it may be valuable in certain situations but not in others.

■ Also like other genres, there is constraint as well as room for flexibility associated with the five-paragraph essay. Ask students how they might find flexibility in the form: What could they alter that would allow their five-paragraph essay to still be effective in an appropriate situation (such as a standardized test)? For each suggestion, help students understand how aspects of that genre—situation, roles, purpose—might be shifted by their alteration. Also, ask how the response to a more innovative, less rigid use of the genre might draw different responses from readers. Be sure to note the effects of such actions as moving the thesis somewhere other than the introductory paragraph, of including more or fewer than three body paragraphs, of shifting topic sentences to the middle or end of paragraphs. It is possible to find examples of these "altered" forms to use in class to help students see the results. I have found many samples of varied paragraph structure in books like *Seabiscuit* (Hillenbrand) and *Walking the Bible* (Feiler). *Newsweek* and *Sports Illustrated* offer articles that exemplify alterations in expectations normally associated with five-paragraph essays.

■ In "Muddying Boundaries: Mixing Genres with Five Paragraphs," I show examples of how to destabilize the form of the five-paragraph essay by inserting different text structures into its standard format. In the following example, taken from the article, the italicized words are additions to a student paragraph from a paper on whether San Francisco or Stamps was a better place for Maya Angelou to grow up (students were responding to *I Know Why the Caged Bird Sings*). The paragraph lacks a typical topic sentence or concluding sentence; it uses lists and an ad as content; it does, however, still focus on making a single point and provides evidence in support of that point—an expectation for paragraphs in this genre.

> *San Francisco: cable cars, the Golden Gate Bridge, winding roads down steep hills, Ghirardelli Square, fog, Chinatown, mimes and musicians on the sidewalk, the wax museum, Fisherman's Wharf.* San Francisco was very open to new ideas, which resulted in a less segregated community. Because of the intermixing of races, the inhabitants were accustomed to different types of people and respected different beliefs and customs. *Stamps: Black Stamps and White Stamps, cotton pickers, dust, baskets full of white people's laundry, segregated schools, the Sheriff on his horse, hiding, fear.* Stamps was a small town and set in its ways. In many respects, when compared to San Francisco, it was behind the times. There were major divisions between races, and as a result, they rarely interacted with one [another]. During Maya's eighth grade graduation a white man spoke to the graduates and their families. He spoke of all the wonderful new equipment the "white" school would be receiving. He assured them that they wouldn't be left out. He promised them new sports and home economics equipment. This is one example of how the different races in Stamps were expected to pursue different occupations. The whites were able to choose from numerous careers and had many more chances to succeed in life. On the other hand, the best job a black could obtain was a cotton-picker, washwoman, butler or maid. In San Francisco because of the little segregation, many jobs were open to all races and more opportunities were present. *Wanted: Trolley ticket taker. Training provided. Some high school required. All eligible applicants apply at 443 Southern Ave.* (Dean, "Muddying" 54–55)

After seeing such paragraphs that destabilize the rigid structural expectations for the five-paragraph essay, have students discuss the consequences the choices have: Is it still a paragraph that would fit in a five-paragraph essay? Does it do what it is supposed to do in its situation? How does it change (if it does) reader and writer roles? Would such flexibility be unacceptable in some situations? Why or why not? Such discussion helps students augment what might be impoverished theories of genre by helping them see that the underlying ideas of logic and coherence in the five-paragraph essay may be achieved without the rigid form.

■ Have students explore the alternative paragraphs discussed in the lesson; they should practice destabilizing their own five-paragraph essays by applying some of those possibilities to their own writing. As they make choices, give them opportunities to have peer responses to their choices so that they can begin to sense readers' potential reactions.

■ Students should reflect on their learning from this experience; have them write a cover letter for their paper in which they describe the ways they altered the format of the five-paragraph essay and the ways they maintained it. They should also reflect on the effects created by their alterations and when and where these might be problematic. By doing so, they should show their understanding of genre as more complex than a form and as responding to situation—a move away from the rigid theory of genre they may have begun the assignment with.

READING SHAPES WITHIN GENRES

This application begins with the concepts of text structures and patterns. Brian Paltridge thinks of *patterns* in writing as "internal discourse patterns" (74); he and others see these internal patterns in broad categories related to purpose—narration, description, persuasion. Christine M. Tardy and John M. Swales refer to such arrangements as a text's "internal rhetorical structure" (567) and see them as more specific organizational features—such as cause-and-effect, chronology, problem-solution. For my students, I refer to broad purposes as *patterns* and organizational arrangements as *structures* to explain these concepts. The following application should help students recognize how these organizational structures and patterns work together to create various kinds of texts; furthermore, understanding these building blocks of genres can help them as readers and writers. Text structures and patterns can help them read a genre as the writer intended, but they can also help them read it for their own purposes. "Hyper-reading," a term used by James Sosnoski to describe characteristics of reading that have developed from perusing online texts, describes how readers often choose different paths through a text, depending on their individual purposes. Helping students understand these reading practices, and the ways they are allowed or constrained by text structures and patterns, can benefit them as users of texts. Awareness of text patterns and structures can help students enact effective communication by making them more aware of the subtle shapes, beyond the more evident forms, within the genres they use.

■ Show picture books that combine text patterns in obvious ways. One example is books in the Magic School Bus series, which combine fictional stories with factual paragraphs (written as mini-reports on the page) or definitions of related terms—narration and a variety of expository text structures. *Snowflake Bentley,* by Jacqueline Briggs Martin, has a more subtle form of the same idea, with a story as the primary text and more research-oriented text in sidebars: direct quotes, facts, explanations that add to the story events. Other possible titles to use for exploration are listed in Figure 3. Have students delve into these texts, looking specifically for different text patterns and structures and probing how they work with and against each other, contributing to a whole. As an example, a page from Nicola Davies's book *Ice Bear: In the Steps of the Polar Bear* has this primary text: "OUR people, the Inuit, call it NANUK. White bear, ice bear, sea bear, others say. It's a bear, all right, but not like any other! It's a POLAR BEAR, made for our frozen world!" (7). On the facing page, we find the following subtext: "Polar bears have longer necks and legs than their closest relatives—brown or grizzly bears" (6). Ask students to consider how these two texts differ. What is the effect when readers choose to read one text pattern without the other? What difference might that make to the writer? Let students investigate a variety of samples and theorize about the specific effects of the different text patterns as well as the overall result of such reading on the writing and communication of ideas. How does each text pattern communicate? How does the use of mixed text patterns contribute to various ways of reading the text?

■ After students have explored text patterns in these picture books so that they understand the concept, have them examine other genres that blend text structures so that readers don't have the choice of skipping or reading one text. A picture book that works well for making this transition is Susan Goldman Rubin's *The Yellow House: Vincent Van Gogh and Paul Gauguin Side by Side*, because it combines comparison-contrast with description and narration in a single flow. Movie or book reviews are also good examples because they contain summary (chronological, narrative-like), analysis (using examples), and evaluation (stating opinion). Have students use highlighters of different colors to identify the various text structures within the genre (Dean, *Strategic* 60). Discuss with them what they learned about how the text structures blend and work together to create the overall effect of the genre.

■ When students have completed their exploration, have them reflect on how learning about text structures and patterns can benefit them both as readers and as writers in the future.

WRITING WITH TEXT STRUCTURES

Once students understand that genres have internal structures, it can be useful for them to comprehend that some genres use a variety of structures to accomplish the action of the genre. Although the following ap-

Cheney, Lynne. *America: A Patriotic Primer.* New York: Simon and Schuster, 2002.

Cole, Joanna. *The Magic School Bus: Inside the Earth.* New York: Scholastic, 1987.

Davies, Nicola. *Ice Bear: In the Steps of the Polar Bear.* Illus. Gary Blythe. Cambridge, MA: Candlewick, 2005.

———. *One Tiny Turtle.* Illus. Jane Chapman. Cambridge, MA: Candlewick, 2001.

Hicks, Peter. *You Wouldn't Want to Live in a Wild West Town! Dust You'd Rather Not Settle.* Illus. David Antram. New York: Franklin Watts, 2002.

Kurlansky, Mark. *The Cod's Tale.* Illus. S. D. Schindler. New York: Putnam's, 2001.

Romanek, Trudee. *Achoo! The Most Interesting Book You'll Ever Read about Germs.* Illus. Rose Cowles. Toronto: Kids Can Press, 2003.

Wright-Frierson, Virginia. *An Island Scrapbook: Dawn to Dusk on a Barrier Island.* New York: Aladdin Paperbacks, 2002.

Figure 3. Picture Books with Obvious Text Patterns

plication uses a diary for the basic genre, other genres—a letter or commentary, for example—also could be used to accomplish the same objective. The application presented below developed from an idea from one of my preservice teachers, Margaret Clark.

- Begin by having students write diary entries for themselves for the previous day. Ask them what they wrote about and how they knew what to write as a diary entry. Ask students how diary entries are different from other kinds of writing—poems, essays, reports, for example. Students should at least identify the personal nature, the content about daily activities, and the informal language that are typical of the genre. Be sure to have them also identify the situations, purposes, and subject positions associated with diaries.

- Bring in real diaries from pioneers or people from other times, so students see how diaries from the past not only contain personal information but also provide insights into the time and culture of the writer.

  – This site has diary entries by Daniel Boone: http://www.early america.com./lives/boone/index.html.

  – This site has diary entries of John Bradbury, a British man traveling in America during the early 1800s: http://www.xmission. com/~drudy/mtman/html/bradbury.html.

  – This site has links to a number of diaries and journals from early America: http://www.over-land.com/diaries.html.

With the historical diary entries, have students identify, in addition to the personal details, what they learn about the time and culture of the writer so that they see how information about the context and culture are woven into the entries.

■ Next, read *Diary of a Worm* and *Diary of a Spider* (Cronin) to students. Discuss the books and what they do. How does the author use the genre of a diary to establish a specific position for the reader—and the writer? What are those positions? Why would the author use a diary for her book—what does she expect readers to anticipate because of the genre she has chosen?

■ Read each book again, this time having students take note of the facts about worms or spiders in it (how many legs a spider has) and the information that is not based in reality (worms go to school). List all the facts on the board. Then, in another column, list the events that are fictional. Discuss how the entries in the book are like those in a diary—that they show daily life and personal attitudes and feelings, problems, and joys. Make sure students see how the diary entries function not only as diary entries but also contain cultural or personal information just as the historical diary entries do. Ask students to identify the different text structures used to convey the worm's or spider's ideas. After investigation, they should notice the following: lists, reflections, retelling of events, dialogue, and dreams, among others. This should help them begin to see that diaries, like many genres, have varied structures within the action that is taken by each diary entry.

■ Give students the assignment to research an animal or object that they can then report on using the diary format, taking a first-person stance and speaking from a personal perspective. Within the diary, though, they will need to include three different text structures as entries: a list, a reflection, and a short informative paragraph in a reversal pattern.

■ Give students time to pick a topic and freewrite on what they already know about the topic before they conduct their inquiry.

■ Provide some suggestions on note-taking strategies. Remind them that notes are a genre with usefulness in the world of school and out of it, too. When they are researching a large purchase, for instance, they might want to keep notes on their options—the price, features, gas mileage, and safety ratings for several models of used and new cars—to help them make their decision. They can practice for that task by keeping notes as they conduct inquiry for this project.

■ Next, give them tips on keeping track of source information so they can include a bibliography with their project. Again, a bibliography or reference list is a genre—it has a situation and a purpose. As part of your instruction in documenting source information, it's a good idea to talk about the way the genre of a bibliography acts in the situation of a research-based paper and the relationships it establishes.

- When students have an idea for what questions they will need to consider during inquiry, how to find sources, and how to keep track of information they learn, give them time to conduct inquiry.

- As part of inquiry, require each student to conduct an interview, either in person or through email, with someone who knows the topic. You can help students practice this genre by encouraging them to consider the situation of the interview, its purpose, and the roles the students and experts play.

- When students have gathered sufficient information, provide them with a selection of lists. Help students explore them and determine their functions (keeping track of information), their situations (a busy day), and their characteristics (particularly parallel structure). After they have done that, they should decide what information they have that would be best presented in a list and a situation in the diary that would best frame that list. Then, have them draft the entry.

- Next, provide several short reflections. Again, have students consider their functions, situations, and characteristics. Have them decide what information they have that would be best presented in a reflection and a situation in the diary that would best frame that reflection. Then, have them draft the entry.

- Finally, introduce the reversal informative paragraph, a strategic option for informative paragraphs. Again, looking at examples is a good way to help students understand the concept behind the reversal structure, an application modified from *The Allyn and Bacon Guide to Writing* (Ramage and Bean). The reversal structure can be found in many places if teachers are on the lookout. It's a "this is what everyone thinks, but this is what you don't know" approach that begins with the common view of a topic and then either explains what is untrue about that common view or extends it. Give students some examples to help them understand it as a strategy for presenting information in an informal way, more conducive to a diary. By contrasting encyclopedia entries with examples such as the ones below, students can understand how reversal writing sets up different relationships through its tone and structure. Students could compare, for example, an encyclopedia entry on alligators with this reversal passage on the same topic from an article by Natalie Angier in the *New York Times:*

To the casual observer, an adult alligator afloat in an algae-dappled
pond, its six-foot body motionless save for the
sporadic darting of its devilish amber eyes, | Common view |
might conjure up any number of images, none
of them fuzzy-wuzzy. A souvenir dinosaur. A log with teeth. A
handbag waiting to happen.

For Dr. Daphne Soares, however, a neuroscientist at the University
of Maryland, an alligator looks like nothing
so much as a big, amphibious and grievously | Introduces unexpected |
misunderstood kitten. Sure, it sports thick | perspective |
scales and bulging bony knobs called
osteoderms rather than fur, and 80 teeth to the house cat's 30, and
a tail that, as Dr. Soares learned from per- | Back to what readers |
sonal experience, can dislocate your jaw with | know and expect. |
a single whack.

But just look at the chubby | The unexpected perspective that will be |
belly, the splayed legs, the | developed now as the writing contin- |
sunny smile that never sets! | ues—this is the reversal. |

And here's another example from *A Field Guide to Pigs: How to Identify
and Appreciate 36 Breeds* (Pukite) that students could compare to more
straightforward reporting:

Pigs oink. In a perfect world, this probably would be enough to
appreciate pigs for all their wonders. In this day
and age, though, pigs occupy a more humble | Common view |
place, a bit off to the side of the more glamorous
farm animals. . . . Unappreciated though they are, pigs are truly
great animals with lively personalities and a | Reversal |
complete lack of manners. (10)

When students understand the concept of the reversal—its tone and patterns as well as the participant roles—have them decide what information they have that would be best presented in a reversal and a situation
in the diary that would best frame it and then draft the diary entry.

   ■ Have students finish their diary by using other information they
have found in more traditional retelling-of-a-day's-event patterns, then
peer evaluate and revise. Help them write the bibliography, framing it
as a genre, not just as a form: What is its situation? What is the action it
carries out in that situation? What role does the writer have in the relationship that the genre performs?

   ■ Have students write reflections wherein they consider the different roles they had to take in writing the diary, the list, the reflection,
the reversal, and the bibliography. How did these roles differ, if they did?

What did students notice about the different stances required for each genre and text structure? How do the various genres, text structures, and text patterns frame and present information differently? How might students apply what they learned about roles and stances to their future writing?

COMBINING GENRES

Several writers have espoused the value of the multigenre research paper (see Figure 4). It offers many options for teachers and students to explore topics and write about them in engaging ways, and, because genres represent ideologies and modes of acting, they can provide a variety of lenses for viewing the world. As such, examining a single subject through multiple genres can help students see that subject differently. As Marie C. Paretti notes, "this understanding of genre as a way of knowing provides insight into one of the central values of having students develop a single idea in multiple genres. . . . These genres potentially provide students with a richer understanding of an idea because students can use one genre as a way to step outside the epistemological framework of another" (122). With this perspective in mind, a multigenre format can sometimes be considered an opportunity for students to use the varying stances required of different genres to create a multivocal paper—one that loses the monologic voice associated with a traditional research paper. If it can do that, it can be extremely beneficial to students.

Michelle Tremmel makes the following observation about the additional value of multigenre papers in helping students develop as writers: "What is most important about multigenre writing is not form and procedure, where those people writing about multigenre papers have, for the most part, focused their attentions so far, but rhetorical decision-making that can allow students to examine rhetorical relationships and social actions through genre and to explore the multigenerity and intertextuality of all texts" (40). I see her point—in the concept. In practice, however, the multigenre paper assignment doesn't always live up to its potential. Too often it has resulted in a collection of artifacts that might resemble a variety of genres but leaves students with a limited notion of genre: genre as form. If teachers neglect to teach the full concept of genres, not only will students fail to see genres as more than forms—thus perpetuating a "container view of genre" (Bawarshi, "Genre Function" 339)—but they will also not benefit from seeing the different perspectives on a subject that writing in a variety of genres can foster.

Allen, Camille A. *The Multigenre Research Paper: Voice, Passion, and Discovery in Grades 4–6.* Portsmouth, NH: Heinemann, 2001.

Allen, Camille A., and Laurie Swistak. "Multigenre Research: The Power of Choice and Interpretation." *Language Arts* 81 (2004): 223–32.

Davis, Robert, and Mark Shadle. "'Building a Mystery': Alternative Research Writing and the Academic Act of Seeking." *College Composition and Communication* 51 (2000): 417–46.

Dickson, Randi, with Jon DeGraff and Mark Foard. "Learning about Self and Others through Multigenre Research Projects." *English Journal* 92.2 (2002): 82–90.

Edwards, Sarah. "Multigenre Teaching as Student Empowerment." *English Leadership Quarterly* 25.4 (2003): 2–6.

Grierson, Sirpa T. "Circling through Text: Teaching Research through Multigenre Writing." *English Journal* 89.1 (1999): 51–55.

Grierson, Sirpa T., with Amy Anson and Jacoy Baird. "Exploring the Past through Multigenre Writing." *Language Arts* 80 (2002): 51–59.

Hamblin, Lynda. "Voices in the Junior High School Classroom: Lost and Found." *English Journal* 90.1 (2000): 80–87.

Johnson, Cheryl L., and Jayne A. Moneysmith. *Multiple Genres, Multiple Voices: Teaching Argument in Composition and Literature.* Portsmouth, NH: Boynton/Cook, 2005.

LeNoir, W. David. "The Multigenre Warning Label." *English Journal* 92.2 (2002): 99–101.

Moulton, Margaret R. "Cookie." "The Multigenre Paper: Increasing Interest, Motivation, and Functionality in Research." *Journal of Adolescent and Adult Literacy* 42 (1999): 528–39.

Putz, Melinda. *A Teacher's Guide to the Multigenre Research Project: Everything You Need to Get Started.* Portsmouth, NH: Heinemann, 2006.

Romano, Tom. *Blending Genre, Altering Style: Writing Multigenre Papers.* Portsmouth, NH: Boynton/Cook, 2000.

———. "Prior to Publishing: Word Work." *Voices from the Middle* 8.1 (2000): 16–22.

———. *Writing with Passion: Life Stories, Multiple Genres.* Portsmouth, NH: Boynton/Cook, 1995.

Slack, Delane Bender. "Fusing Social Justice with Multigenre Writing." *English Journal* 90.6 (2001): 62–66.

Starkey, David, ed. *Genre by Example: Writing What We Teach.* Portsmouth, NH: Boynton/Cook, 2001.

Figure 4. Resources for Background on Multigenre Research Papers

Unity can also be a problem when students write multigenre papers. W. David LeNoir notes this problem in his classroom experience: "Although the multigenre format encourages the use of widely disparate forms of writing—poetry, essays, articles, and letters, to name a few—

simply assembling them in the same document serves no purpose. The point of a multigenre paper is to convey a unified message through means that reflect the richness of the experience, so this unity must be reflected not only in the content of the individual elements, but also by how they work together" (100). Tom Romano addresses the problem of unity by teaching "skillful repetition" and sees the solution as helping writers learn to be more attentive to readers' needs. As he says (and I have found to be true), "multigenre papers require a great deal of readers. So much is implicit, so little explicit that multigenre papers can be quite a cognitive overload" (*Blending* 149). Tremmel asserts that the concept of uptake—an understanding of how genres respond to each other and to their situations—as essential to creating this sense of unity (36). If students envision the multigenre research paper as a scrapbook or a simple collection of items, they miss the point of it and don't consider readers' needs—an aspect of genres that they should think about.

If teachers can help students understand genres in theoretically sound ways, a multigenre paper is an effective tool for students to practice working meaningfully with genres. Some teachers have students focus only on specified genres as a way to help students learn more about those genres and control the kind of uninformed use that can lead to genre-as-formula thinking. Other teachers provide students with more options by requiring a few specified genres (which the class learns about together) and allowing some genres to be chosen by students as needed.

Two teachers I have worked with, Amy Anson and Jacoy Blair, developed a rationale card to help students consider genre choices carefully. Their rationale card is partly represented in the "Multigenre Reality Check" shown in William Strong's book *Write for Insight: Empowering Content Area Learning, Grades 6–12* (155). In the rationale, students document for each genre what information came from research, what came from inferences from research, and what was imagined or made up. Because they must identify what sources they used for each genre, they are more likely to move away from the one-source-per-genre tendency that sometimes occurs with this kind of project. Additionally, students describe why they selected each genre: what about the genre made it an appropriate choice for the information it presents. Using such metacognitive and accounting measures helps students learn more about both writing and using genres in the multigenre project and reduces the risk that they'll end up thinking about genres as only forms.

The resources in Figure 4 are helpful to teachers who want to have students write multigenre papers. The application that follows is elaborated in many of those sources.

■ Begin by having students look at some texts that use a multigenre format so that they get an idea of what the project entails. Give students time to investigate the models and then ask them questions to make sure they see how the texts work, how the different genres present information, and how they work together to create a unified whole. Possible texts are *Our Eleanor: A Scrapbook Look at Eleanor Roosevelt's Life* by Candace Fleming and *Crossing the Delaware: A History in Many Voices* by Louise Peacock.

■ Next, have students select a topic of interest to research and write about. Have them conduct inquiry, keeping track of sources and acquired information.

■ When students are ready to begin drafting, give the assignment requirements. I suggest asking for a small number of genres, including one short research report in traditional style, no longer than three pages. In my experience, asking for or allowing too many genres makes the project unmanageable for many students and often results in a limited view of genres. Other than that, depending on the kinds of topics students have selected (projects on famous people would suggest different genres than projects on historical events), use the opportunity to expose students to one or two genres they may not have encountered. Follow processes that involve exposure to multiple sample texts, discussions about the situations those genres work in, and examinations of the ways they position users. This exploration should include opportunities to see how genres work and why some information might be appropriate for one genre and not another. Tom Romano, for example, presents his class with two pieces of writing about Count Basie—an encyclopedia entry and a poem (*Blending* 19). By contrasting the two, students are able to see the many ways genres can present information as well as the varied tones they take—and the different perspectives and content they both allow and constrain.

■ Provide staggered due dates for separate parts of the project. This works especially well if you are providing instruction about and exposure to certain genres as students work; students can then plan to have their versions of that genre submitted in at least a draft form prior to the whole project's due date. Certainly, by the end of the project, students should have had a chance to look at its pieces and consider how to arrange them to allow for the genres to interact with each other in the most effective ways.

■ Give students time to reflect in writing on what the project taught them about their subject, about writing, and about genres. Have them consider how the various genres privilege different positions and how they both constrain and allow certain perspectives. How might such learning benefit them in the future?

WRITING MINI-ETHNOGRAPHIES

Ethnography is a way to look at a culture; Wendy Bishop describes it as "a representation of the lived experience of a convened culture" (3). Reiff, citing Beverly Moss, explains that "the main purpose of the ethnographic genre is 'to gain a comprehensive view of the social interactions, behaviors, and beliefs of a community or a social group'" ("Mediating" 42). Ethnographies, therefore, are both genres and studies of genres' effects in situations. Certainly the social nature of genres lends itself to the social research that is ethnography—genres both act in and represent the action of the research into how people interact. Extending that idea, Reiff calls ethnography a "meta-genre" because "it refers both to the *written genre* or rhetorical performance whose typified patternings reflect and reveal the investigative purpose of a community of researchers and to the *research methods* or 'actions' that give rise to this genre, requiring researchers to observe and participate in the actions of the community being investigated" (41; emphasis added). Thus, using genres as a lens into a community provides ways to practice genres as both products and processes.

Writing ethnographic research teaches about genres because of how it draws attention to participant roles in enacting genres. Reiff notes that this research "casts students . . . into dual roles as both participants in the community and observers of the community's interactions" (42). Furthermore, conducting research for ethnography requires students to use genres for authentic purposes, which provides them with clear connections between genres and contexts and helps them see genres as actions more than forms. Reiff lists the following possibilities for genres that can aid in conducting ethnographies: students could "write letters to seek permission to observe groups, or they might write proposals for their research or research plans and agendas. During the research, they draw on several genres as tools: field notes, journals or activity logs, project chronologies or summaries, progress reports, interview transcripts, even maps. And once the research is completed, they may practice additional genres that the situation warrants such as thank you notes, self-assessments, peer assessments, or abstracts" (47). Bishop adds surveys and questionnaires as other possible genres for inclusion in such a project. Certainly, any of these methods contribute to research but also teach about genres as students use them for authentic purposes.

When ethnographic methods—taken from anthropology, sociology, and other social science fields—combine with writing research, we find what Bishop refers to as "a complicated hybridization" (4). She provides the following criteria to guide ethnographic writing research:

- Ethnographic writing research is ethnographic in *intent*.
- Ethnographic writing research is participant-observer–based inquiry.
- Ethnographic writing research studies a culture from that culture's point of view.
- Ethnographic writing research uses one or more ethnographic data-gathering techniques.
- Ethnographic writing research gains power to the degree that the researcher
  a. spends time in the field
  b. collects multiple sources of data
  c. lets the context and participants help guide research questions
  d. conducts analysis as a reiterative process. (35)

Helping students understand these criteria moves them toward conducting effective ethnographic writing research.

A full ethnography is more than can be accomplished in a secondary classroom setting, but Bishop's mini-ethnography project is a way to gain the benefits of connecting genre theory with ethnographic research. She defines mini-ethnographies by explaining them in reference to larger ethnographies: "Macroethnographies report research on multiple sites and involve larger or longer projects than do microethnographies, which can report on the culture of the single classroom, the single learner, and even the single learning event. . . . Students in my classroom conducted what I called mini-ethnographies. . . . These were brief person-based studies that encouraged them to undertake basic ethnographic practices: document examination, interview, and observation" (73). What follows is a plan for guiding students through a mini-ethnographic research project. I heartily suggest reading Bishop's book to get a good idea of what these projects look like. Although the ethnographies described there are longer and more complex than those likely to be conducted by secondary students, they still give a good view of the genres involved.

- To help students understand what a mini-ethnography is, begin work on one as a class. Select a short genre that you have access to and that functions in a situation students would be familiar with. A pass to the counseling office or a referral slip for detention works well. Students need to know that the intent of this investigation is to understand a culture better—not make judgments about it.

■ Begin by having students describe the context and situation associated with the genre you've selected for the class investigation. Make notes to keep for the write-up.

■ After students have a good sense of the context of the genre, have them investigate and analyze the genre in small groups. The following questions, suggested by Clark, are possible prompts for student analysis:

> What purpose does this genre serve?
> What are the features of this genre?
> How do its particular generic features serve its purpose?
> For whom is this genre written?
> What role must the writer assume in writing this genre?
> Whose interests does this genre serve? ("A Genre Approach" 9)

When students have considered all aspects of the form, have them speculate on "what the rhetorical patterns reveal about the community—its purposes, its participants, and its values, beliefs, and ideologies" (Devitt, Bawarshi, and Reiff 554). Discuss findings with the whole class.

■ Next, have students interview users of the genre from as broad a perspective as possible. So, for instance, if students are investigating a detention referral form, they should interview teachers who fill it out, students whose actions are written up on it (as well as those who've never had one filled out for them), and administrators who have to deal with the incidents reported on it. Teach them about interviewing, develop questions as a class, and have each student conduct one interview. Then, with the findings they report in mind, conduct further analysis of the genre to determine how it represents the community's actions, values, and beliefs.

■ In compiling the ethnography as a class, use collaborative writing. Have some students write up the description of the situation where the genre acts. Others can compose the analysis of the genre; still others can describe what the genre tells about the community that uses it. Combine all the pieces so students see the purpose of the mini-ethnography: to explain how a genre reflects the actions and beliefs of a community—not to judge it. Since an ethnography isn't a genre many students might have had exposure to, model the writing first to show them its characteristics: the first-person voice, the dual stance (both observer and participant) that enables supposition as well as assertion, the content that addresses situation and genre, *and* insights into community. Help students learn to focus on the important implications rather than everything that might be considered.

■ Next, have students select a genre to begin their own mini-ethnographies. Since they should be participant-observers, it might be best to have them start with genres that function in communities they are already participants in. Have them write what they know of the community and situation surrounding the genre and begin the analysis of the genre itself with questions to guide them. Because one way that working on mini-ethnographies benefits genre learning is through the reliance on multiple genres during inquiry, make sure students keep journals or progress reports of their processes and data. Thus, they learn the value of these kinds of genres.

■ Next, students should interview other users of the genre to collect data from multiple perspectives. Bishop acknowledges that one challenge to ethnography as a research method is the way it is too often limited to a single technique (13). Adding interviews to the individual questioning and examination increases the credibility of the conclusions students draw. Give further instruction on developing questions for interviews, arranging for them, keeping track of the information given, and documenting the information in a transcript (another functional genre).

■ To help students further determine the ideologies of their target genre, have them use questions for critiquing a genre from the application in this chapter. At this point and other points during the inquiry process, be sure students repeat the analysis, refining it and exploring pertinent questions that arise.

■ Make sure students work through the writing process—drafting, engaging in peer review, revising, and editing. When they've completed the process, have them reflect on what they learned about genres from the mini-ethnographies: How will they look at genres differently in the future? How will they use them differently?

ANALYZING A WRITING SITUATION

One way students can learn about genres is by analyzing a writing situation and drawing conclusions about it and the roles the writer is expected to take. This will also benefit them by improving their performance in those situations, particularly when the situations carry high stakes, such as testing. As Anne Ruggles Gere, Leila Christenbury, and Kelly Sassi assert: "Most writing is writing on demand" (5). In other words, writers most often write because some person or situation requires it, not because they personally feel compelled to do so. If we think of writing as situated and as prompted in some way, understanding the situation and responding appropriately are important skills regardless of the circumstances.

This application makes use of uptake, of situation, and of analysis and applies to texts that instigate writing as much as those that respond to those instigations. Teachers might want to consider addressing how responses could comply with or resist the expectations established in the prompt and the possible consequences of either choice.

In his book *The Testing Trap: How State Assessments Control Learning*, George Hillocks Jr. addresses this issue of conformity to or violation of the expectations for the genre of a large-scale writing test when he recounts a student's "antigenre" response to an Illinois standardized test prompt (Peters 200). As Peters notes, an antigenre can help a writer "articulate what she knows about a topic in a new way" but it also "reconstitutes the voice of the writer" and works subversively to "functionally [satisfy] the social purpose of the genre it resists" (201). By employing an antigenre, a writer "reinvents" the original genre's conventions (200).

In Hillocks's example, the student wrote what the state published as an example of "best" writing but what was, in reality, "a parody of the sugary content and form . . . that the test [typically] elicits" (114). Because the expectation for this genre (at least in this situation) was content that would fit in a five-paragraph format, the student used that format to introduce fake evidence that actually disproved his thesis. His readers, situated to look only at form, missed the student's resistance—and fakery—altogether. The student saw through the role he was expected to play and used the genre for his own purposes: to poke his finger in the eye of the testers. An understanding of genre can help students clarify their roles in testing situations; furthermore, if they recognize the consequences of resisting or adhering to a genre's expectations, they can develop their critical thinking abilities, which will obviously serve them well in any writing situation. As they begin to question genre forms and content, they will also become more sensitive to the ways others around them use genres to take advantage of expected roles and situations.

■ Gather writing prompts from other teachers and classes, from previous state tests, from journals with calls for manuscripts, from creative writing sites calling for submissions, or any other appropriate places for use in class analysis. The wider the variety the better. It is possible to find some prompts online, as listed below, but they are extremely decontextualized and may not give students enough information to analyze the situation. Students and teachers could perhaps establish contexts, such as large-scale testing or a history class, to better use these prompts.

– This site has simple prompts for young students: http://www.manatee.k12.fl.us/sites/elementary/PALMASOLA/wexpository.htm.

– This site has past brief prompts from Nevada's state writing test that would need to be contextualized for students: http://www.writingfix.com/dailytesttakingpromptgenerator.htm.

■ Introduce this investigation process by having students freewrite about past situations when they might have responded inappropriately to a writing assignment or test prompt. If they've never had that experience, they should write about how they have avoided it. What did they do? How did they know how to respond to writing prompts they were given?

■ After students have finished with this task, encourage them to share their experiences as a way to show how being able to analyze a writing situation can affect how successfully they approach any writing task given by someone else—at school, in tests, or at work.

■ As a class, use one of the following sets of questions or a combination of them to analyze a writing assignment or test prompt. Give students a copy of the assignment or prompt and place the questions on the board or a screen so the class can work through the questions together; this practice will help students understand how to find the answers in the assignment or prompt on their own later. Be sure to explore not only the answers to the questions but also the implications of those answers. For instance, if no audience is specified, what should a student assume? How much do the assumptions depend on the situation—a final class assignment, a college entrance exam? And if the prompt says that the audience is the mayor, but the students know the test will be read by scorers and not the mayor, what decisions does that mean they should make for their writing?

In *Scenes of Writing*, Devitt, Reiff, and Bawarshi provide a list of questions, some of which are given below, that students can use to analyze a writing assignment. The questions help students locate the assignment in a situation.

1. Setting: What kind of course is this assignment for? Is this one of a set of assignments?

2. Subject: Does the assignment specify a subject? If not, what subjects are most appropriate? Whatever subject I choose, how am I being asked to treat it?
3. Writers: What kind of role does the assignment ask me to take? What sort of stance should I take?
4. Readers: What kind of information does the assignment provide about the readers? What else do I need to know about the readers for me to address them effectively?
5. Purposes: Other than to get a grade, why am I writing this assignment? What does the teacher want me to gain from this assignment? What do I want to gain?
6. Genre Features: Are there certain expectations about organization and format? About style? Given the role I will be taking on, my readers, and the subject matter, what style will be most appropriate? (198)

Using an approach that combines rhetoric with a little bit of genre, Gere, Christenbury, and Sassi suggest a set of questions that could be used to analyze the writing prompt for a test, although they could also be used to analyze a writing assignment. Their list includes the following:

1. What is the central claim or *topic* called for?
   Do I have choices to make with regard to this claim or topic? Will I need to focus the claim or topic in order to write a good essay? What arguments can I make for this claim? What do I know about this topic?
2. Who is the intended *audience*?
   If named specifically, what do I know about this particular audience? If the audience is implied or not identified, what can I infer about it? In either event, how might the expectations of this audience affect my choices as a writer?
3. What is the *purpose* or *mode* for the writing task?
   Is the purpose stated or must it be inferred? What is this writing supposed to accomplish (besides fulfilling the demands of the prompt or assignment)? What does the goal of this writing suggest about the mode (narration, exposition, description, argument) or combination of modes that I should consider in responding?
4. What *strategies* will be most effective?
   What does the purpose or mode suggest about possible strategies? Of the strategies I am comfortable using—like examples, definitions, analysis, classification, cause and effect, compare and contrast—which will be most effective here? Are there any strategies, such as number of examples or type of support, that are specified as required?
5. What is my *role* as writer in achieving the purpose?
   Have I been assigned a specific role, like *applicant* or *representative*? If I have not been assigned a specific role, what does the prompt or assignment tell me about the level of expertise I should

demonstrate, the stance I should assume, or the approach I should take? (67)

■ Have students break into small groups and use selected questions to continue analyzing additional prompts to build understanding of varying situations and develop stances and strategies for successfully accomplishing the writing tasks. If groups have the same prompt, they could compare findings. If they have different ones, they can present to the rest of the class how they would respond to the prompts and receive feedback about aspects they may have missed.

■ When students have a grasp of using questions to analyze the assignments or prompts, provide possible responses that don't meet the expectations of the prompt in some way. In other words, if the prompt asks for a persuasive response, give students a personal experience that might connect to the idea of the prompt but that doesn't actually do what it requests. For instance, some state tests ask for students to persuade a reader that school should or should not be held only four days a week. An inappropriate response would be a narrative about a time when parents kept a student home from school on a Friday so they could all go to an amusement park and not have to wait in long lines. Most state testing sites have strong and weak examples that could be used for this exploration. Have students work in small groups or individually to ascertain where the writer misread the expectations and what could be done to bring the response into compliance. Also have them consider if they can read the differences as resistance or as a misreading of the situation's expectations—and how they know.

■ Finally, have students practice writing in response to a prompt or assignment by first analyzing it and then writing in accordance with their analysis. Have peers evaluate the writing for its effectiveness in responding to the prompt and the situation. In their reflections, have students attribute their choices to the expectations they found through analysis. If they chose to resist expectations, have them explain why—and what possible outcomes they could anticipate from their resistance.

RECOGNIZING INTERTEXTUALITY

In discussing intertextuality, Bazerman makes this vivid observation: "We create our texts out of the sea of former texts that surround us, the sea of language we live in. And we understand the texts of others within that same sea. . . . Sometimes as readers we consciously recognize where the words and ways of using words come from and at other times the origin just provides an unconsciously sensed undercurrent. And sometimes the words are so mixed and dispersed within the sea that they can no longer be associated with a particular time, place, group, or writer. Nonetheless, the sea of words always surrounds every text" ("Intertextuality" 82–83). In helping students understand how texts relate to each other, teachers can provide a number of experiences. One is to examine writing prompts from a variety of settings—large-scale tests, English classes, history or science classes, essay contests—and determine the different expectations for language, ideas, and arrangement in each situation. Students should find that each prompt will be somewhat responsive to the "sea of words" associated with the particular situation it responds to. Bazerman suggests finding a news article and letter to the editor on the same topic and looking at the ways the two different genres respond to each other and to other texts and ideas around them (94). The application that follows is another way to help students explore intertextuality while they work with a variety of genres.

- After they read a short story or novel, have students find help wanted ads for jobs that they find interesting. Looking online, students can enter a zip code and get a number of possibilities that include job descriptions as well as characteristics the employers are seeking.

- When they have selected an ad that contains enough criteria for them to know what the employer is looking for, have them examine several résumés. They should use questions such as those listed in other applications in this book to help them recognize the rhetorical purpose of a résumé as well as its response to specific situations—in other words, they should see that résumés are not all alike, even those from the same person.

- After students have a good sense of the ways résumés respond to situations, have them select a character from the literature they have read to respond to the help wanted ad. They should review the job characteristics as well as the character's traits, as revealed in the literature. Then have them write a résumé for that character in response to the posted position. They will probably have to create false addresses and phone numbers—even some previous work or educational experience—but the information presented in the résumé should be consistent with what is revealed about the character in the literature. So, for instance, if students used characters from *The Odyssey* in this way, they could say that Odysseus had experience managing a crew and delegating tasks and that he was used to traveling in his work, so travel wouldn't be a problem for him. They could not say, however, that he had experience in an office or as a shopkeeper. Students could have Circe apply for work as a nurse because of her experience with herbs, for example, but they couldn't claim she had expertise as a mechanic since nothing in the story would support that contention.

■ Although some online applications no longer require anything other than a résumé, many still require a cover letter. Ask students, once they have the résumé completed, to write a corresponding cover letter. Have them examine and analyze examples of cover letters to see how they work and what relationships they establish between the writer and the addressee.

■ When students have drafted both letter and résumé, have them work as partners with others who have used the same characters, so that they can get feedback on the accuracy of their use of evidence from the literature. Have them also consider the résumés and letters as texts and look for ways they can accomplish the purposes of those texts more effectively. Have them revise.

■ After they have finished revising to their satisfaction, have students work with others who selected different characters. Have them compare the ways the help wanted ads position the applicants—is the job for a well-qualified manager or an entry-level worker?—and how well their résumés and cover letters respond to that positioning. If their documents don't meet the requirements very well—if the ad requires many years of nursing work or a pharmacy degree but Circe has only a limited knowledge of herbs—what possible outcome could they expect?

■ Finally, have students examine their own and others' texts for the ways they respond to each other. In other words, how do the résumés change for different jobs? And how do cover letters adjust to the different characters and job situations? Have students reflect in writing about experiences with intertextuality beyond the classroom and how their learning through these activities might benefit them as they use genres to act outside of school.

Appendix A: Teaching Questions

If we teach genres in schools, what are the pros and cons of explicit teaching of genres?

Even with a belief that limited instruction in genres can occur in schools, some theorists feel that explicit teaching can focus only on forms, a problematic pedagogy. Coe refers to such instruction, related to teaching the five-paragraph theme, when he speaks of "the problem with teaching genres dogmatically, statically, as structures" ("Teaching" 163). Richardson suggests a similar view of explicit teaching when he poses two questions related to its expected goals: "How far does conscious knowledge of structure make for more effective performance in writing?" and "Does emphasis on structure detract from emphasis on meaning?" (133). Certainly if teaching focuses on texts simply as forms, the dynamic, social, and ideological aspects of genres are lost. But explicit teaching does not necessarily mean a teacher-directed, formulaic approach to genre.

Even when it doesn't become that type of approach, other objections to explicit teaching include Freedman's strong hypothesis that such teaching doesn't do what teachers hope it will: "Explicit teaching is unnecessary; for the most part, not even possible; and where possible, not useful. . . . Further, whenever explicit teaching does take place, there is risk of overlearning or misapplication" ("Show" 226). She cites Sondra Perl's 1979 study that showed explicit teaching leading to students overgeneralizing—and thus not learning what was intended ("Do" 206). Berkenkotter and Huckin note another reason some people reject explicit teaching—they "negatively associate the explicit teaching of genres with the prescriptive *rhetorical modes* approach that had students reading 'exemplary' essays by linguistically and rhetorically mature writers . . . as models for student writing" (*Genre* 153). Even if teachers use a variety of examples to help students see genres as flexible, students might still misapply teachers' intentions.

However, some theorists believe explicit teaching is necessary because of issues of access. Hicks notes that the acquisition of "school-based literacies in the wider sense of formal, institutional modes of talk and social action only seems natural because of the similarity of their primary Discourses to the secondary Discourses of schooling" (464). In other words, those who argue that students don't need explicit teaching may be thinking only of those students whose home lives predispose them to easily acquire the genres of schooling and, eventually, of power. Bill Cope and Mary Kalantzis agree, noting that "students from historically marginalized groups . . . need explicit teaching more than students who seem destined for a comfortable ride into the genres and cultures of power" (7).

Coe extends this view and makes the point that many students, not only those without access but also those that don't do well in school, might benefit from explicit teaching:

> But even though writers can learn to write without such explicit knowledge, might it be helpful? Would such knowledge help teachers teach or writers write? Might explicit genre knowledge help some students, perhaps especially some of *those who presently fail*? Would some explicit genre knowledge help other students master genres more quickly? Could teachers with explicit genre knowledge better facilitate learning (by whatever method)? People learned to swim for millennia before coaches explicitly articulated our knowledge of how to swim, but kids today learn to swim better (and in less time) on the basis of that explicit knowledge. The same can be said about most athletic and craft skills. Might it be true for writing as well? ("Teaching" 158–59)

As Herrington and Moran point out, explicit teaching makes the "rules . . . visible" (11). Although not everyone needs genres to be so delineated, there may be some students who do—and they would benefit from explicit instruction.

Some theorists see the inclusion of explicit teaching as a more complex issue, recognizing that the approach may have value besides simply helping students to produce texts because it can assist them in developing genre knowledge beyond the textual level, what Gee describes as meta-knowledge, the ability to talk about performance: "Acquisition and learning are different sources of power: acquirers usually beat learners at performance, learners usually beat acquirers at talking about it, that is, at explication, explanation, analysis, and criticism" (146). Devitt makes a similar point: "Explicit teaching may not be necessary for people to produce acceptable texts with appropriate generic forms, then, but it may be necessary for people to perceive the purposes of those forms and their potential ideological effects" (*Writing* 195–96). Explicit teaching may benefit students' knowledge about the abstract aspects of genre more than the concrete ones. As Fahnestock points out, "students are not going to recognize regularities in texts (and genres are only definable by regularities) if they do not expect regularities or do not know what counts as a significant regularity worthy of imitation" (270). Joseph M. Williams and Gregory G. Colomb go so far as to claim that implicit teaching may hide ideologies from students because it leaves them for students to discover on their own. Thus, some explicit teaching may be necessary for students to fully comprehend genres as more than forms.

Freedman sees some value to future learning from explicit teaching that helps students gain genre meta-knowledge: "Explicit teaching may be able to 'raise the consciousness' of some learners so that they will later notice and hence acquire features in meaning-focused input" ("Show" 243). Martin, Christie, and Rothery, arguing that implicit teaching really means leaving students with the limited choices of their personal experiences and comfort levels, suggest that explicit teaching widens students' array of options, enabling them to have better tools to achieve their goals (77). To come to an understanding of genres that will benefit them beyond school, students might need some explicit instruction in school about the nature of genres and how to understand them. Devitt shows she is clearly aware of the problems of explicit teaching— but she sees value in it anyway:

> Teaching language and genre explicitly risks enforced conformity to formula, but such teaching has the potential reward of helping students integrate their understanding of rhetoric . . . with the linguistic and generic forms that they produce. Having seen the extent to which genre shapes language, I am reluctant to leave my students ignorant of those effects. Language, genre, and writing interact, sometimes in quite small and subtle ways. To ignore that fact is to mystify writing, to allow genre and situation to encourage linguistic conformity on writers unaware, and to deny students access to a better understanding of why as well as what they write. It may be dangerous to teach expected forms, but it may be even more dangerous not to teach them. (*Writing* 213)

Part of the answer to the question of explicit teaching's value lies in defining what explicit teaching does or can mean, what its goals are, and what it looks like. Explicit teaching has been described differently, sometimes pejoratively, depending on the perspective of the speaker. Chapman addresses the common view as well as a more flexible one when she explains that "explicit instruction need not imply a rigid, structuralist approach. Rather, it can entail a conscious attempt to focus students' attention on particular aspects of writing rather than expecting students to discover them on their own. The degree of explicit instruction we provide then is something with which each of us must struggle on an ongoing basis, with every new group of students—indeed, with each writing situation" (487). By considering explicit teaching as a continuum—"the degree of explicit instruction"—teachers may see more flexibility, more alternatives for instruction. Cazden considers it important to find methods to "achieve flexible competencies from explicit teaching" (6). One option, she notes, is the use of a variety of models that show a range of genre characteristics so that students and teachers move away from finding formula in a single model. Other researchers suggest that a rich classroom context, significant discussion, and exploration of ideas are all part of what they consider explicit teaching, although others consider these activities implicit. Certainly we have to consider that explicit teaching is not necessarily the rigid, form-based pedagogy some envision. Neither is it necessarily a single, teacher-centered approach.

In response to the debate about explicit teaching, Coe finds a middle ground: varying instruction to match the needs of students and the genres they use. "To what extent writers and writing students should be explicitly conscious of the genres they use is more variable, as is the extent to which students can usefully be told what the defining features of a genre are, the extent to which they will be better off if they reinvent the genre through an experiential process or through their own analysis. And so our pedagogy should be comparably variable" ("Teaching" 163).

As Herrington and Moran's research shows, there is "evidence that writers acquire genre knowledge both consciously and unconsciously. This would suggest that teachers can teach genre explicitly and implicitly" (66). Although Carol A. Donovan and Laura B. Smolkin's review of research found that "direct teaching of [a variety of text structures] improved understandings of, and abilities, in those genres," their implications for instruction suggest a similar conclusion: "Greater exposure to, and meaningful experiences with, reading and writing a range of important genres . . . would be beneficial" (139). We may teach some genres explicitly—and others implicitly, through authentic experience—and at other times take a genre awareness approach. To elaborate on Chapman's assertion: we can teach genres, teach about genres, teach through genres, teach with genres, teach in genres (473). All genre learning can be beneficial.

More recent research assumes, then, that some balance of implicit and explicit teaching is needed for students to acquire genre knowledge. The question now being asked is "what combination of experience and explicit instruction best facilitates learning of new language forms" (Purcell-Gates, Duke, and Martineau 8). Research findings suggest that this combination may shift for the types of genres being learned (41) and that some developmental factors may help determine what works best (42). Because, as researchers note, language—and therefore writing—is multidimensional, some aspects of it may be more "amenable to explicit instruction" than others (41). Teachers should be aware of this issue so as to make the most effective instructional decisions they can. Certainly the inclusion of explicit teaching is not simply a right-or-wrong proposition.

Does a genre approach limit creativity and individual expression?

Because of its focus on writing's social aspect, some critics worry that a genre approach can limit personal expression. J. R. Miller acknowledges that an emergent idea of community could be "troublesome," that it could possibly "devalue individual rights" ("Rhetorical" 72). Concern about either emphasis—social or individual—is important, because both positions fail to attend to the necessary balance of the two, as Joseph Harris points out: "We do not write simply as individuals, but we do not write simply as members of a community either" (275). A clear concept of the relationship of the individual to the community is essential to creativity, as Kaufer and Geisler, in reviewing the literature on novelty in academic writing, find: "Newness is less a property of ideas than a relationship between ideas and communities, and less an individual trait than a regularity of communal life and structure" (288). Thus, an individual's self-expression can actually be enhanced by a relationship to a community, by understanding a need for balance between the social and the individual.

Despite this assurance, the pressure to conform to the community, to genre expectations, is a complicated matter. Devitt addresses some of this complexity when she refers back to Freadman's metaphor of genre as etiquette: "In addition to genres constraining people because they are functional and make rhetorical sense, then, generic etiquette constrains people if they want to belong to a group" (*Writing* 148). A desire to belong, to show insider status, can be a powerful motivation to follow expected behaviors and to diminish or eliminate individual expression. Bazerman argues that the pressure may not only be a desire to belong: "What we might feel as the weight of living up to the expectations of a particular genre is in fact rather the reminder of all the complexities at stake in the form. The pressure of genre is not of conformity so much as of response to complexity, and insofar as we feel drawn to or seek traditional formal solutions, those standardized forms provide a means to begin to address the situation in a focused way" ("The Life" 23). If conformity to generic expectations eases the way to performing a genre, to belonging to a community, it is understandable how compelling such conformity would be—and why teachers would need to be aware of this pressure and find methods to help novice writers handle it. Bawarshi suggests that the way to help writers "transgress genres" must be "connected to the knowledge of the social motives that these genres maintain and articulate" (*Genre* 92). So understanding the social aspects of genre can be both constraint and a way to resist constraint.

Some critics worry that the constraints of the genres themselves, not just the community's influence, could be problematic for individual expression. Such criticism focuses on two misconceptions: that genres involve only constraint and that constraint is always a bad thing. The first misconception derives partly from neglecting current theory about genres and instead focusing on genres as fixed forms. It is true that constraints are part of any genre. Bakhtin claims that our use of language, despite the potential for adaptability, is never totally free because it always involves prior use and audience expectations; for Bakhtin, language is always part of a "chain of other utterances" (69). But limitation is only a part of a genre. The individual's use of it brings in another aspect: "we must see both constraint and choice as necessary components of genre" (Devitt, "Language" 45). Chapman asserts that most "genres are sufficiently open-ended to allow for individual choice, creativity, and voice [and making them is] . . . very much an individual creative process as well as a social one" (471). Clark, reporting on a presentation made by David Bleich at CCCC in 1997, points out that "creativity can only exist within the context of genre, because genres become more effective and revitalized when their formal properties are altered by the incorporation of the personal" ("Genre" 251). Jason Wirtz phrases the combination of constraint and choice in a unique way: "infinity within a finite space" (24). Choice within constraint. Since people can also choose from among several possible responses (genres) to begin, there is also choice before constraint.

Regarding the second misconception, Devitt resists the idea of genre as enabling choice because that "perspective still implies that constraint is bad and choice is good" ("Genre as Language" 45). In fact, she argues, "creativity theory suggests that creativity derives from constraint as much as from freedom" (*Writing* 138), a point Coe agrees with: "Generic forms are factors in the creative processes of speaking and writing" ("An Arousing" 183). As with language, some expectations are necessary for communication—and creativity—to occur. Constraint, in and of itself, is not bad.

Additionally, genres are constraining (and flexible) in varying degrees—and for varying reasons. As Devitt explains, "even the most rigid genre requires some choices, and the more common genres contain substantial flexibility within their bounds" ("Generalizing" 580). Bawarshi, using Medway's term "baggy genres," notes also that some genres "allow for more resistance and playfulness" than others (*Genre* 92). Indeed, Bakhtin theorized (and Bawarshi says essentially the same thing) that the most flexible are the "artistic" genres, and more standardized genres, such as those from business and the military, are less so (63). As Devitt later claims, "variation is permitted to the degree that it does not negate either function or appropriateness" (*Writing* 149). With poetry, more variation is expected and therefore allowed. With a business document, function and appropriateness are much more prescribed—and therefore much more limited.

In addition to the nature of the genres themselves, flexibility may also be related to our familiarity with genres: "The better our command of genres, the more freely we employ them, the more fully and clearly we reveal our own individuality in them (where this is possible and necessary)" (Bakhtin 80). Bawarshi, in addressing an individual's options for flexibility, asserts that resistance—"to be recognized and valued as resistance and not misinterpretation or, worse, ignorance—must be predicated on one's knowledge of a genre" (*Genre* 92). We must conclude, with Devitt, that "genre enables writers to make choices as much as or more than it requires writers to conform" (*Writing* 153)—but these choices have personal and contextual limitations.

Because of the balance between choice and constraint, between the social and the personal, genres can actually promote creativity and individuality. Wendy Bishop and Hans Ostrom assert that it is "the very nature of . . . contemporary genre theory . . . to blur, dissolve, or at least cross boundaries; it is to violate decorum and trouble hierarchies" (Introduction xii). Certainly, such blurring can be both an impetus for and a result of flexibility and choice. Because, as Freedman and Medway note, "the most powerful texts cross generic and cultural boundaries," writers can find ways to create more interesting and individually representative responses by functioning within genres ("Introduction" 16). Writers can conform to genre expectations, can stretch the boundaries of them, or they can resist them and use another genre altogether. When they do, what do they say? How does the rejection of the expected also convey meaning? And how does that resistance eventually change the genre and the situation? Far from reducing or eliminating creativity and individuality, a genre approach can promote them.

Appendix B: Terms and Definitions

Several terms used in genre theory have a range of meaning, and in this section, I address some of those terms and their various uses.

What is the difference between texts and genres?

As Kress notes, "for some theorists *text* and *genre* are identical; for others, they are not" ("Genre and the Changing" 464). To complicate matters, some theorists also use *text type* interchangeably with *text*. As far as I can determine, there are three possibilities for the use of *text* and *genre* in the literature related to genre theory.

1. *Texts* as *genres,* evidence of a social action. This seems to be how Coe thinks of the connections between these terms when he says that "a genre is neither a text type nor a situation, but rather the functional relationship between a type of text and a type of situation" ("New Rhetoric" 197). In this use, *text* and *genre* seem interchangeable—and both represent social action. It also seems to be how Bazerman uses *text* here: "Each successful text creates for its readers a social fact. The social facts consist of meaningful social actions being accomplished through language, or speech acts" ("Speech Acts" 311).

2. *Texts* as documents; *genres* as actions. In this use, a text represents the enactment of the action a situation requires, and that text incorporates aspects of the situation. Kress seems to employ this meaning when he states the following: "A number of quite distinct matters go to make up what a text is: genre certainly is one" and then adds age, gender, the form of language, and other factors related to situation ("Genre and the Changing" 464). In this definition, a genre appears to be an aspect of situation, and the text is the document produced as a result of social exchange within that situation.

3. *Genre* as document and *text* as text type, when text type represents "rhetorical modes such as 'problem-solution,' 'exposition,' or 'argument,'" or is representative of forms "of internal discourse patterns, irrespective of genre" (Paltridge 74). Coe refers to this definition of *text* as text type when he writes, "The new genre theories vary significantly, especially in size of text type they associate with genre" ("New Rheto-

ric" 198). Instead of *genres*, Grabe calls these general patterns of organization *macro-genres* and names two broad examples: exposition and narration. Bhatia calls the same thing *rhetorical/generic values:* "essentially independent of any grounded contextual constraints" (281). Then Bhatia identifies a second level, *genre colonies*, which he describes as "loosely contextualized in terms of socially recognizable patterns" (he gives the example of promotional genres) (281), and finally a third level he labels *genres* and defines as individual genres that "are more typically and narrowly grounded in typical sociorhetorical contexts" (282). He cites sales letters, job applications, advertisements—what others might call texts.

So, the answer to the question? It depends. And, it seems to me, it partly depends on the perspective on genre theory that the theorist holds. Those interested in equity for students, looking at genres as stable and fixed, and with linguistic backgrounds tend to favor the last definition, although they might also see *text* as document. Those more inclined to see genres as social acts that only tangentially include written documents would lean more toward *text* as action.

What is meant by context?

Context is also a challenging term because it, too, is used differently by various theorists. Although it is important to all rhetorical theories of genre, its definition is complicated, as Devitt explains: "It is difficult to specify what context includes. Not everything about the surrounding environment (the temperature, what is happening in the next block) is relevant for the language use being considered, and some things outside the surrounding environment (potential readers, previous texts) are relevant" ("Generalizing" 577).

Responding to the difficulty of identifying exactly what context entails, Devitt suggests that the "concept of discourse community developed usefully in composition theory for several purposes, among them to help specify the overly vague abstraction of 'context' and to call attention to the social nature of texts" (*Writing* 36). So some theorists prefer to use *discourse community* to narrow and refine the concept of context. Referring to Swales, Devitt notes these characteristics of discourse communities:

- "common public goals"
- "mechanisms of intercommunication . . . primarily to provide information and feedback"
- use of "one or more genres" with "some specific lexis"
- "a threshold level of members with a suitable degree of relevant content and discoursal expertise." (39)

Because "the concept of discourse community privileges discourse above other group activities" and "disguises the social collectivity that shapes the very nature of the group and its discourse," Devitt feels that "it emphasizes too heavily the role of discourse in constructing groups and not enough the role of groups in constructing discourse" (*Writing* 39). Thus it is an inadequate term to describe the interaction of genres and group and context. Berkenkotter and Huckin address another problem with using *discourse community* as an explanation of *context*: "Asserting a relationship between the concept of genre and that of discourse community is a slippery proposition, because neither concept refers to a static entity" ("Rethinking" 497). So, elements of discourse community help explain context but do not do so satisfactorily for many theorists.

Russell's term "activity system" is used by some theorists to make context less abstract: "An activity system is a unit of analysis of social *and* individual behavior, something like a discourse community, but it allows us to think about tools without confining ourselves to discourse and about people who interact purposefully without confining ourselves to the warm and fuzzy notion of community" (82). This explanation seems to encompass group interactions that move beyond discourse, and therefore it addresses concerns that the concept of discourse community doesn't acknowledge. Devitt also notes that "activity theory discourages simple dialogism in favor of multiple voices and undercuts rigid dualities" in the way it portrays the interactive nature of groups (*Writing* 47). However, she also acknowledges that it is limiting in its portrayal of "genre more as a tool than as an action, and it diminishes the role of people in creating and using genres" because of its emphasis on systems (47).

Since other terms are inadequate to address the myriad aspects that contribute to context, theorists break down the concept and consider several levels or aspects of environment for genres. Coe suggests three: "We should look at the tangible patterns of discourse (including regularities of both structure and subject matter), the rhetorical situation (with some emphasis on both purpose and strategy), and the context of the situation (with some emphasis on function)" ("Teaching" 166). For him, context would include a broad level, what others might call the activity system or discourse community; an intermediate level, which has to do with general purpose and approach; and a narrow level, the immediate environment, the specifics of a particular use of a genre. With this explanation, he also addresses limitations of considering only rhetorical situation as context, since that designation holds less regard for the social relationships inherent in context than contemporary genre theory posits.

Taking a slightly different approach, Devitt establishes three different kinds of contexts that have more to do with conceptual influences than distance of influence: context of culture, context of situation, and context of genres. "Each kind of context has both a material and a constructed reality, for what makes them 'contexts' is the extent to which people give them significance. . . . These contexts of situation, culture, and genres act simultaneously and interactively within a genre, and genre sits at the nexus of such interactions" (*Writing* 29). Context, then, may be described and defined in multiple ways. It must, however, address a multitude of influences on generic actions and the people performing genres. Keeping in mind the host of contextual factors at play in genre performance is probably the best way to consider context.

What do we call related genres?

Because genres are related to each other—they grow out of each other and overlap and interact within and between groups and activities—theorists also address these genre relationships. Considering genre relationships offers insight into other aspects of genre theory beyond intertextuality—how genres are historical, dynamic, and connected and how they benefit a group's identity and interactions. As Devitt notes, "genre sets help the community to cohere and define itself" (*Writing* 56). Bazerman describes the relationship between genres and communities like this: "Acts are carried out in patterned, typical, and therefore intelligible textual forms or genres, which are related to other texts and genres that occur in related circumstances. Together the text types fit together as genre sets within genre systems, which are part of systems of human activity" ("Speech Acts" 311). Bazerman sees a genre set as "the collection of types of texts someone in a particular role is likely to produce" (318). Devitt defines it as "the set of genres that exists within a particular 'sphere of activity' or group" (*Writing* 54). She gives an example of "a memo announcing a meeting" and the corresponding "minutes of that meeting" as pieces that might constitute part of a genre set (55).

Within a genre set, there may exist an "alpha genre"—what Bawarshi describes as a genre that functions as a meta-genre—to define the "atmosphere" and establish a unity among the genres of a set (*Genre* 180). A syllabus could be an alpha genre since it functions not only as a meta-genre, establishing a way of being and unifying other genre activities, but also as a genre itself. Thus, a genre set can accomplish the activities of a group, and the alpha genre exists as a primary genre that instigates the actions contributed by other genres in that set.

According to Bazerman, genre systems encompass genre sets: "A genre system is comprised of the several genre sets of people working together in an organized way, plus the patterned relations in the production, flow, and use of these documents" ("Speech Acts" 318). Devitt says that Bazerman's notion of a genre system is more like what she calls "genre sets" (*Writing* 56). Devitt sees genre systems in a more structured way. She calls them the "set of genres interacting to achieve an overarching function within an activity system" (56) and notes that "each genre system can be described in terms of a particular activity it accomplishes" (57).

Devitt then expands her idea of genre relationships by adding the genre repertoire: "the set of genres that a group owns, acting through which a group achieves all of its purposes, not just those connected to a particular activity" (*Writing* 57). A genre repertoire seems to be more flexible in its interactions and connections that a genre system, according to Devitt's use of the term. As she explains it, a repertoire is "also a set from which participants choose, a definer of the possibilities available to the group" (57). In attaching these terms to contexts, she hypothesizes "that communities more often operate through genre repertoires, collectives more often through genre systems or genre sets, and networks more often through single genres interacting with other genres only in the largest context of genres" (58). Despite the different uses of this terminology, the general idea is to consider how genres relate—to each other and to their situations—and to consider the ways such relationships influence our use and understanding of genres.

Appendix C: New Directions

Meta-genre

According to Janet Giltrow, a meta-genre is an "atmosphere of wordings and activities, demonstrated precedents or sequestered expectations—atmospheres surrounding genres" (195) or "guidelines . . . for the production of a genre" (190). Bawarshi describes the meta-genre as a unifying principle that "sanctions and regulates" the use of genres in "an activity system" (*Genre* 99). That is, as people interact with genres, they assume subject positions appropriate to the actions of the genres. When they interact with multiple genres, they may assume multiple, sometimes conflicting, subject positions. A meta-genre—insider knowledge—can help outsiders as they take up these positions.

When students come to a class for the first time, they must learn to position themselves in the discourse expected for that class. As Bawarshi explains, "because of training, experience, attachment, and/or proclivity, a writer may certainly feel more 'at home' in one genre position than another" (*Genre* 99). Because of this inclination toward a particular subject position—what Bawarshi calls a default position—writers may continue to act with genres "when they no longer serve their user's best interests" and "will resist certain genres that conflict in some way" with those positions (99). Thus, despite the principles that guide writing for a specific college course, some students maintain the subject position expected in a narrative instead of taking on the subject position expected for that course—an analytical or evaluative position, for example. Meta-genre, the way a teacher talks about expectations and presents instruction, might establish the classroom context to explain and support appropriate positioning for students, allowing them to move from one position to another with understanding.

Uptake

Freadman mentions uptake by name in her article "Anyone for Tennis?" and Bakhtin seems to allude to it when he observes that the "pauses between utterances are, of course, not grammatical but real" (74). Uptakes are the spaces in between genres. Taking an approach more from the genre as practice end of the continuum, Freadman argues "that 'genre' is more usefully applied to the interaction of, minimally, a pair of texts than to the properties of a single text" ("Uptake" 40). What Freadman wants to address with uptake is the "bidirectional relation that holds between this pair" (40)—in other words, the way one text responds to another and the actions that occur because of that interaction. Bawarshi, who also investigates the concept, defines *uptake*

> as the ideological transactions that configure, normalize, and activate meaning relations within and between systems of genres. Knowledge of uptake is what helps us select, define, recontextualize one genre in bi-directional relation to another so that one genre becomes a normalized response to another. Knowledge of uptake is knowledge of what to take up, how, and when: when and why to use a genre, how to select an appropriate genre in relation to another, how to execute uptakes strategically and when to resist expected uptakes, how some genres explicitly cite other genres in their uptake while some do so only implicitly, and so on. ("'Uptake'" 3)

From this description, teachers can see that the way students respond to an assignment—what they do and how they do it—is an example of uptake.

Freadman describes uptake as "how we get from one to the other" ("Uptake" 44), so we come to see that there are certain signals genre users select or do not select that help them when they perform response genres. Gillian Fuller and Allison Lee note that uptake sequences (in work, in school writing) "become interiorized"; that is, we may not see all the signals that occur in the spaces between genres. Freadman gives an example of asking her father if she could mention his name in a piece of writing in connection with a specific incident. He replied that he would write his version of it for her—which was not at all what she expected in response to her request. Instead, her father contextualized her request against previous requests (for more than simple approval for his name to be mentioned). She concludes, "Uptakes . . . have memories" ("Uptake" 40): they respond to more than simply the immediately preceding genre.

Because of this uptake memory, students sometimes perform genres inappropriately: We assign analysis; they write summary. We provide the prompt, and they write something that makes us wonder what they heard us say or what they read into the assignment. Uptake can help account for some of those inappropriate responses. Students are responding, taking up our genre request, by contextualizing it with all previous memories of other teachers and other school writing—and perhaps, even memories beyond those, situations that we may not be aware of. As Bawarshi notes, "genre knowledge does not *necessarily* imply a corresponding uptake knowledge, since uptakes are informed by discursive resources that may exceed genre knowledge" (*Genre* 5–6). Students might know some genres of school writing, but not precisely what we mean by our specific genre request.

Bawarshi also asserts that "uptake profiles configure the range of permissible ways genres can be taken up—their horizons of expectation" ("Uptake" 4). In other words, there are a limited number of appropriate ways to take up (or respond to) a genre. At CCCC in 2006, Bawarshi used James Frey's *Million Little Pieces* as an example of inappropriate uptake, explaining that its label as a memoir caused the media uproar—we expect a *memoir* to be true, but we expect a *novel* to contain fiction. When a memoir isn't fact, it exceeds its uptake profile by moving outside the realm of permissible responses. In their book *Scenes of Writing*, Devitt, Reiff, and Bawarshi comment on another such case, Rigoberta Menchu's 1983 memoir (181–82). After winning the Nobel Prize and bringing about social change, the memoir was shown to be elaborated—events either did not actually occur to her or were exaggerated. The ensuing controversy then, too, is evidence of the possible reactions when genres exceed uptake profiles. Freadman explains that "the uptake text has the power not to so confirm this generic status, which it may modify minimally or even utterly" ("Uptake" 40). It could be argued (as Devitt and her colleagues point out) that Menchu deliberately used the uptake profile of a memoir—the readers' expectations for personal experience and truthfulness—to bring about social change. Certainly that is an option. Genres may move outside the boundaries of their uptake profiles, or range of appropriate responses; when they do, as in these cases, users need to be aware of the range of possible consequences.

Border genres

In the literature associated with genre theory, terms such as *borderline genres, boundary genres, crossover genres,* and *genres created by insiders for outsiders* suggest some of the ways that new theories of genre are being complicated. As Freedman and Medway observe, "as genre theory evolves . . . it becomes obvious that more and more text is generically problematic" ("Introduction" 16). In other words, we are beginning to realize that the ways texts act and interact for, with, and between communities are not easily explained, much less categorized. *Border genres* describes these more complex interactions that occur between communities.

Border genres obscure traditional definitions of community but support the idea of genres as ways of acting and as representative of ideologies. As Devitt, Bawarshi, and Reiff note, "although the borders of communities are more permeable and fluid than the community meta-phor suggests, clashes of knowledge and perspective still result when specialists and nonspecialists meet, clashes that have consequences in terms of how participants interact, perform their actions, and produce certain effects in the world" ("Materiality" 544). Giltrow describes some-thing similar when she, referring to Russell's work with activity systems, speaks of meta-genres thriving where "intersecting activity systems" meet (203). She agrees with Russell that "inadequacies in our sense of situation or context" lead to a tendency to focus on text and "neglect . . . or underestimate" context (202). Border genres complicate theory and practice, but they also address aspects of genre theory that may have been inadequately considered to this point.

In exploring border genres, Devitt, Bawarshi, and Reiff specifically mention genres that are written by insiders to be used by outsiders: tax forms, ballots, and jury instructions (548). We might include writing prompts, because, as Bawarshi points out, "the prompt, like any other genre, organizes and generates the conditions within which individuals perform their activities" (*Genre* 127). It provides cues for appropriate action in the classroom: "the writing prompt not only *moves* the student writer to action; it also *cues* the student writer to enact a certain kind of action" (127). Because teachers (insiders) create the prompt for students (usually outsiders), the writing that students undertake as a response (the uptake) fits within the concept of border genres. Understanding this con-cept (along with uptake and meta-genre) can help teachers understand better the reasons students respond to the prompts the way they do and can help teachers improve their writing prompts.

Genre effect

In a paper presented at CCCC in 2006, Bastian discussed genre effect: "the various assumptions and beliefs we have about genre itself that affect how we understand individual genres working" (3). She explains that regular "interactions and experiences" with a variety of genres make them seem more similar than different, thus creating the genre effect: "beliefs that genres achieve only one primary action, that textual differ-ences do not matter, and that similar situations are equivalent" (5). Johns, seeing the same thing, notes that "students' theories . . . are often in di-rect opposition to the genre theorists' complex ideas" ("Destabilizing" 239). In other words, the genre effect means that students become desen-sitized to the implications associated with genre—with the implicit ide-ology, with the effects of the textual choices, with the range of subject positions available, with the potential for resistance. Indeed, Paré suggests that this response—unquestioned acceptance—is partly a result of the nature of genres themselves: "the automatic, ritual unfolding of genres makes them appear normal, even inevitable; they are simply the way things are done" (59).

The genre effect occurs, then, partly because of the roles genres create for participants: "mobilizing of genres within jurisdictional parameters produces both texts and desiring subjects" (Fuller and Lee 222). Such subject positions can cause participants to accept—without question—the ideologies of a genre. As Coe describes the process, the genre effect occurs partly because the roles created by genres force participants to neglect some aspects of genre in favor of others: "teaching students or other people to pay attention to what is important in a situation, task, or text inevitably involves a judgment about what is less important or not important, and inevitably deflects their attention away from what has been judged less relevant, sometimes to the point where they no longer even notice it. If these people then move to another situation, task, or text, the mode of perceptions, interpretation, and response they have so carefully learned sometimes produces an inadequate perception and thus an incompetent response" ("New Rhetoric" 202). Thus, our use of some genres—and the subject positions associated with them—may not just predispose us to favor certain genre responses and subject positions but may actually interfere with our making effective responses in new situations. Bastian acknowledges that the genre effect does not eliminate the possibility that students—really, all of us—will be critical rather than passive subjects, but she does argue for helping students become aware of the genre effect by having them work first with less familiar genres, ones that possess "little relevance for success in their daily and academic lives" (8). By doing so, she asserts, students are more likely to understand the genre effect and therefore become less complacent subjects in the genres they do perform more regularly.

References

Andrew-Vaughan, Sarah, and Cathy Fleischer. "Researching Writing: The Unfamiliar-Genre Research Project." *English Journal* 95.4 (2006): 36–42.

Angelou, Maya. *I Know Why the Caged Bird Sings.* New York: Random House, 1969.

Angier, Natalie. "Not Just Another Pretty Face." *New York Times* 26 Oct. 2004. 1 Oct. 2007 <http://www.nytimes.com/2004/10/26/science/26croc.html?ex=1256443200&en=c194455917eeb25c&ei=5090&partner=rssuserland>.

Applebee, Arthur N. "Problems in Process Approaches: Toward a Reconceptualization of Process Instruction." *The Teaching of Writing: Eighty-Fifth Yearbook of the National Society for the Study of Education, Part II.* Ed. Anthony R. Petrosky and David Bartholomae. Chicago: U of Chicago P, 1986. 95–113.

Baker, Russell. "Slice of Life." *New York Times* 24 Nov. 1974. Rpt. in *English: Orange Level.* Evanston, IL: McDougal, Littell, 1989. 218–20.

Bakhtin, M. M. "The Problem of Speech Genres." *Speech Genres and Other Late Essays.* Trans. Vern W. McGee. Ed. Caryl Emerson and Michael Holquist. Austin: U of Texas P, 1986. 60–102.

Bastian, Heather. "Creating a Critical Generic Subject in the Writing Classroom." Ts. Conf. on Coll. Composition and Communication Convention. Palmer House, Chicago. 24 Mar. 2006.

Bawarshi, Anis. *Genre and the Invention of the Writer: Reconsidering the Place of Invention in Composition.* Logan: Utah State UP, 2003.

———. "The Genre Function." *College English* 62 (2000): 335–60.

———. "'Uptake' as Mediating Discursive-Ideological Space between Genres." Ts. Conf. on Coll. Composition and Communication Convention. Palmer House, Chicago. 24 Mar. 2006.

Bazerman, Charles. "Genre and Identity: Citizenship in the Age of the Internet and the Age of Global Capitalism." Coe, Lingard, and Teslenko 13–37.

———. "Intertextuality: How Texts Rely on Other Texts." Bazerman and Prior, *What Writing Does* 83–96.

———. "The Life of Genre, the Life in the Classroom." Bishop and Ostrom 19–26.

———. "Speech Acts, Genres, and Activity Systems: How Texts Organize Activity and People." Bazerman and Prior, *What Writing Does* 309–39.

———. "Where Is the Classroom?" Freedman and Medway, *Learning* 25–30.

Bazerman, Charles, and Paul Prior. "Participating in Emergent Socio-Literate Worlds: Genre, Disciplinarity, Interdisciplinarity." *Multidisciplinary*

Perspectives on Literacy Research. Ed. Richard Beach, Judith Green, Michael Kamil, and Timothy Shanahan. 2nd ed. Cresskill, NJ: Hampton, 2005. 133–78.

———, eds. *What Writing Does and How It Does It: An Introduction to Analyzing Texts and Textual Practices.* Mahwah, NJ: Erlbaum, 2004.

Berkenkotter, Carol, and Thomas N. Huckin. *Genre Knowledge in Disciplinary Communication: Cognition, Culture, Power.* Hillsdale, NJ: Erlbaum, 1995.

———. "Rethinking Genre from a Sociocognitive Perspective." *Written Communication* 10 (1993): 475–509.

Bhatia, Vijay K. "Applied Genre Analysis: Analytical Advances and Pedagogical Procedures." Johns, *Genre in the Classroom* 279–83.

Bishop, Wendy. *Ethnographic Writing Research: Writing It Down, Writing It Up, and Reading It.* Portsmouth, NH: Heinemann, 1999.

Bishop, Wendy, and Hans Ostrom, eds. *Genre and Writing: Issues, Arguments, Alternatives.* Portsmouth, NH: Boynton/Cook-Heinemann, 1997.

———. Introduction. Bishop and Ostrom ix–xv.

Bomer, Randy. *Time for Meaning: Crafting Literate Lives in Middle and High School.* Portsmouth, NH: Heinemann, 1995.

Brooks, Kevin. "Reading, Writing, and Teaching Creative Hypertext: A Genre-Based Pedagogy." *Pedagogy* 2 (2002): 337–56.

Bryson, Bill. *A Short History of Nearly Everything.* New York: Broadway, 2003.

Carlson, Nancy. *How to Lose All Your Friends.* New York: Puffin, 1997.

Cazden, Courtney B. "A Report on Reports: Two Dilemmas of Genre Teaching." Working with Genre Conference. Sydney, Australia. 21–23 May 1993. ERIC Document No. ED363593.

Chapman, Marilyn L. "Situated, Social, Active: Rewriting Genre in the Elementary Classroom." *Written Communication* 16 (1999): 469–90.

Clark, Irene. "Genre." *Concepts in Composition: Theory and Practice in the Teaching of Writing.* Ed. Irene L. Clark. Mahwah, NJ: Erlbaum, 2003. 241–83.

———. "A Genre Approach to Writing Assignments." *Composition Forum* 14.2 (2005). 29 March 2006 <http://www.fau.edu/compositionforum/14.2/clark-genre-writing.html>.

Clements, Peter. "Re-Placing the Sentence: Approaching Style through Genre." *Refiguring Prose Style: Possibilities for Writing Pedagogy.* Ed. T. R. Johnson and Tom Pace. Logan: Utah State UP, 2005. 198–214.

Coe, Richard M. "'An Arousing and Fulfilment of Desires': The Rhetoric of Genre in the Process Era—and Beyond." Freedman and Medway, *Genre* 181–90.

———. "The New Rhetoric of Genre: Writing Political Briefs." Johns, *Genre in the Classroom* 197–207.

———. "Teaching Genre as Process." Freedman and Medway, *Learning* 157–69.

Coe, Richard M., Lorelei Lingard, and Tatiana Teslenko, eds. *The Rhetoric and Ideology of Genre: Strategies for Stability and Change.* Cresskill, NJ: Hampton, 2002.

Comprone, Joseph J. "Generic Constraints and Expressive Motives: Rhetorical Perspectives on Textual Dialogues." *Professional Communication: The Social Perspective.* Ed. Nancy Roundy Blyler and Charlotte Thralls. Newbury Park, CA: Sage, 1993. 92–108.

Cooper, Charles R. "What We Know about Genres, and How It Can Help Us Assign and Evaluate Writing." *Evaluating Writing: The Role of Teachers' Knowledge about Text, Learning, and Culture.* Ed. Charles R. Cooper and Lee Odell. Urbana, IL: NCTE, 1999. 23–52.

Cope, Bill, and Mary Kalantzis. "Introduction: How a Genre Approach to Literacy Can Transform the Way Writing Is Taught." Cope and Kalantzis 1–21.

Cope, Bill, and Mary Kalantzis, eds. *The Powers of Literacy: A Genre Approach to Teaching Writing.* Pittsburgh: U of Pittsburgh P, 1993.

Corbett, Edward P. J., and Robert J. Connors. *Classical Rhetoric for the Modern Student.* 4th ed. New York: Oxford UP, 1999.

Cronin, Doreen. *Diary of a Spider.* Illus. Harry Bliss. New York: Cotler, 2005.

———. *Diary of a Worm.* Illus. Harry Bliss. New York: Cotler, 2003.

Davies, Nicola. *Ice Bear: In the Steps of the Polar Bear.* Illus. Gary Blythe. Cambridge, MA: Candlewick, 2005.

Dean, Deborah. "Muddying Boundaries: Mixing Genres with Five Paragraphs." *English Journal* 90.1 (2000): 53–56.

———. *Strategic Writing: The Writing Process and Beyond in the Secondary English Classroom.* Urbana, IL: NCTE, 2006.

Devitt, Amy J. "Generalizing about Genre: New Conceptions of an Old Concept." *College Composition and Communication* 44 (1993): 573–86.

———. "Genre as Language Standard." Bishop and Ostrom 45–55.

———. *Writing Genres.* Carbondale: Southern Illinois UP, 2004.

Devitt, Amy J., Anis Bawarshi, and Mary Jo Reiff. "Materiality and Genre in the Study of Discourse Communities." *College English* 65 (2003): 541–58.

Devitt, Amy J., Mary Jo Reiff, and Anis Bawarshi. *Scenes of Writing: Strategies for Composing with Genres.* New York: Pearson/Longman, 2004.

Dobrin, Sidney I. "Paralogic Hermeneutic Theories, Power, and the Possibility for Liberating Pedagogies." Kent 132–48.

Donovan, Carol A., and Laura B. Smolkin. "Children's Understanding of Genre and Writing Development." *Handbook of Writing Research.* Ed. Charles A. MacArthur, Steve Graham, and Jill Fitzgerald. New York: Guilford, 2006. 131–43.

Drake, Ernest [Dugald A. Steer]. *Dragonology: The Complete Book of Dragons.* Cambridge, MA: Candlewick, 2003.

Ehrenworth, Mary, and Vicki Vinton. *The Power of Grammar: Unconventional Approaches to the Conventions of Language.* Portsmouth, NH: Heinemann, 2005.

Fahnestock, Jeanne. "Genre and Rhetorical Craft." *Research in the Teaching of English* 27 (1993): 265–71.

Feiler, Bruce. *Walking the Bible: A Journey by Land through the Five Books of Moses.* New York: Perennial, 2002.

Fleming, Candace. *Our Eleanor: A Scrapbook Look at Eleanor Roosevelt's Remarkable Life.* New York: Atheneum, 2005.

Foster, David. "The Challenge of Contingency: Process and the Turn to the Social in Composition." Kent 149–62.

Freadman, Anne. "Anyone for Tennis?" Freedman and Medway, *Genre* 43–66.

———. "Anyone for Tennis?" Reid 91–124.

———. "Uptake." Coe, Lingard, and Teslenko 39–53.

Freedman, Aviva. "'Do As I Say': The Relationship between Teaching and Learning New Genres." Freedman and Medway, *Genre* 191–210.

———. "Show and Tell? The Role of Explicit Teaching in the Learning of New Genres." *Research in the Teaching of English* 27 (1993): 222–51.

———. "Situating 'Genre' and Situated Genres: Understanding Student Writing from a Genre Perspective." Bishop and Ostrom 179–89.

Freedman, Aviva, and Peter Medway, eds. *Genre and the New Rhetoric.* London: Taylor, 1994.

———. "Introduction: New Views of Genre and Their Implications for Education." Freedman and Medway, *Learning* 1–22.

———, eds. *Learning and Teaching Genre.* Portsmouth, NH: Boynton/Cook, 1994.

Frey, James. *A Million Little Pieces.* New York: Anchor, 2005.

Fulkerson, Richard. "Four Philosophies of Composition." *College Composition and Communication* 30 (1979): 343–48.

Fuller, Gillian, and Allison Lee. "Assembling a Generic Subject." Coe, Lingard, and Teslenko 207–24.

Gee, James Paul. *Social Linguistics and Literacies: Ideology in Discourses.* London: Falmer, 1990.

Gere, Anne Ruggles, Leila Christenbury, and Kelly Sassi. *Writing on Demand: Best Practices and Strategies for Success.* Portsmouth, NH: Heinemann, 2005.

Giltrow, Janet. "Meta-Genre." Coe, Lingard, and Teslenko 187–205.

Gladman, J. "How to Write a Really Bad Essay." *Oxford Tutor.* 23 Sept. 2007 <http://www.durham.edu.on.ca/grassroots/oxfordtutor/badessay.html>.

Grabe, William. "Narrative and Expository Macro-Genres." Johns, *Genre in the Classroom* 249–67.

Harris, Joseph. "The Idea of Community in the Study of Writing." *Rhetoric and Composition: A Sourcebook for Teachers and Writers.* Ed. Richard L. Graves. 3rd ed. Portsmouth, NH: Boynton/Cook, 1990. 267–78.

Herrington, Anne, and Charles Moran, eds. *Genre across the Curriculum.* Logan: Utah State UP, 2005.

Herron, Howard "Bud." "Cat Bathing as a Martial Art." 23 Sept. 2007 <http://www.tlcpoodles.com/catbath.html>.

Hesse, Karen. *Out of the Dust.* New York: Scholastic, 1997.

———. *Witness.* New York: Scholastic, 2001.

Hicks, Deborah. "Working *through* Discourse Genres in School." *Research in the Teaching of English* 31 (1997): 459–85.

Hillenbrand, Laura. *Seabiscuit: An American Legend.* New York: Ballantine, 2002.

Hillocks, George, Jr. *The Testing Trap: How State Assessments Control Learning.* New York: Teachers College P, 2002.

Himley, Margaret. "Genre as Generative: One Perspective on One Child's Early Writing Growth." *The Structure of Written Communication: Studies in Reciprocity between Writers and Readers.* By Martin Nystrand (with Margaret Himley and Anne Doyle). Orlando: Academic, 1986. 137–57.

Horning, Alice S. *Revision Revisited.* Cresskill, NJ: Hampton, 2002.

Hyon, Sunny. "Genre and ESL Reading: A Classroom Study." Johns, *Genre in the Classroom* 121–41.

Jamieson, Kathleen M. "Antecedent Genre as Rhetorical Constraint." *Quarterly Journal of Speech* 61 (1975): 406–15.

Johns, Ann M. "Destabilizing and Enriching Novice Students' Genre Theories." Johns, *Genre* 237–46.

———, ed. *Genre in the Classroom: Multiple Perspectives.* Mahwah, NJ: Erlbaum, 2002.

———. Preface. Johns, *Genre* i.

Johns, Ann M., Anis Bawarshi, Richard M. Coe, Ken Hyland, Brian Paltridge, Mary Jo Reiff, and Christine Tardy. "Crossing the Boundaries of Genre Studies: Commentaries by Experts." *Journal of Second Language Writing* 15 (2006): 234–49.

Kaufer, David S., and Cheryl Geisler. "Novelty in Academic Writing." *Written Communication* 6 (1989): 286–311.

Kay, Heather, and Tony Dudley-Evans. "Genre: What Teachers Think." *ELT Journal* 52 (1998): 308–14.

Kent, Thomas, ed. *Post-Process Theory: Beyond the Writing-Process Paradigm.* Carbondale: Southern Illinois UP, 1999.

Kohn, Alfie. "Accelerated Direct Success." *English Journal* 91.1 (2001): 36.

Kress, Gunther. "Genre and the Changing Contexts for English Language Arts." *Language Arts* 76.6 (1999): 461–69.

———. "Genre as Social Process." Cope and Kalantzis 22–37.

Kurlansky, Mark. *Salt: A World History.* New York: Penguin, 2002.

Lalli, Frank. "Game Ball: How to Shamelessly Use Your Child to Get an Autographed Baseball." *Reader's Digest* Apr. 2003: 110–12.

Langer, Judith A. "Children's Sense of Genre: A Study of Performance on Parallel Reading and Writing Tasks." *Written Communication* 2 (1985): 157–87.

Larson, Erik. *The Devil in the White City: Murder, Magic, and Madness at the Fair That Changed America.* New York: Vintage, 2004.

Lattimer, Heather. *Thinking through Genre: Units of Study in Reading and Writing Workshops 4–12.* Portland, ME: Stenhouse, 2003.

Lemke, J. L. "Genre as a Strategic Resource." NCTE Convention. Orlando, FL. 18 Nov. 1994. ERIC Document No. ED377515.

Lendler, Ian. *An Undone Fairy Tale.* Illus. Whitney Martin. New York: Simon and Schuster, 2005.

LeNoir, W. David. "The Multigenre Warning Label." *English Journal* 92.2 (2002): 99–101.

Martin, Jacqueline Briggs. *Snowflake Bentley.* Illus. Mary Azarian. Boston: Houghton Mifflin, 1998.

Martin, J. R. "Mentoring Semogenesis: 'Genre–Based' Literacy Pedagogy." *Pedagogy and the Shaping of Consciousness: Linguistic and Social Processes.* Ed. Frances Christie. London: Cassell, 1999. 123–55.

Martin, J. R., Frances Christie, and Joan Rothery. "Social Processes in Education: A Reply to Sawyer and Watson (and Others)." Reid 58–82.

Menchu, Rigoberta. *I, Rigoberta Menchu: An Indian Woman in Guatemala.* Trans. Ann Wright. New York: Verso, 1987.

Miller, Carolyn R. "Genre as Social Action" *Quarterly Journal of Speech* 70 (1984): 151–67.

———. "Rhetorical Community: The Cultural Basis of Genre." Freedman and Medway, *Genre* 67–78.

Munsch, Robert N. *The Paper Bag Princess.* Illus. Michael Martchenko. Toronto: Annick, 1980.

Myers, Nancy. "Genre as Janus in the Teaching of Writing." Vandenberg, Hum, and Clary-Lemon 164–69.

National Writing Project and Carl Nagin. *Because Writing Matters: Improving Student Writing in Our Schools.* San Francisco: Jossey-Bass, 2003.

Paltridge, Brian. "Genre, Text Type, and the English for Academic Purposes (EAP) Classroom." Johns, *Genre* 73–90.

Pang, Terence T. T. "Textual Analysis and Contextual Awareness Building: A Comparison of Two Approaches to Teaching Genre." Johns, *Genre* 145–61.

Paré, Anthony. "Genre and Identity: Individuals, Institutions, and Ideology." Coe, Lingard, and Teslenko 57–72.

Paré, Anthony, and Graham Smart. "Observing Genres in Action: Towards a Research Methodology." Freedman and Medway, *Genre* 146–54.

Paretti, Marie C. "Intertextuality, Genre, and Beginning Writers: Mining Your Own Texts." *Teaching Academic Literacy: The Uses of Teacher-Research in Developing a Writing Program.* Ed. Katherine L. Weese, Stephen L. Fox, and Stuart Greene. Mahwah, NJ: Erlbaum, 1999. 119–34.

Peacock, Louise. *Crossing the Delaware: A History in Many Voices.* Illus. Walter Lyon Krudop. New York: Atheneum, 1998.

Peagler, T. Shane, and Kathleen Blake Yancey. "The Resumé as Genre: A Rhetorical Foundation for First-Year Composition." Herrington and Moran 152–68.

Peters, Brad. "Genre, Antigenre, and Reinventing the Forms of Conceptualization." Bishop and Ostrom 199–214.

Petraglia, Joseph. "Is There Life after Process? The Role of Social Scientism in a Changing Discipline." Kent 49–64.

Pukite, John. *A Field Guide to Pigs: How to Identify and Appreciate 36 Breeds.* New York: Penguin, 2002.

Purcell-Gates, Victoria, Nell K. Duke, and Joseph A. Martineau. "Learning to Read and Write Genre-Specific Text: Roles of Authentic Experience and Explicit Teaching." *Reading Research Quarterly* 42 (2007): 8–45.

Quammen, David. *The Boilerplate Rhino: Nature in the Eye of the Beholder.* New York: Scribner, 2000.

Ramage, John D., and John C. Bean. *The Allyn and Bacon Guide to Writing.* Brief ed. Boston: Allyn and Bacon, 1997.

Reid, Ian, ed. *The Place of Genre in Learning: Current Debates.* Geelong, Victoria, Australia: Deakin University Centre for Studies in Literacy Education, 1987.

Reiff, Mary Jo. "Mediating Materiality and Discursivity: Critical Ethnography as Metageneric Learning." *Ethnography Unbound: From Theory Shock to Critical Praxis.* Ed. Stephen Gilbert Brown and Sidney I. Dobrin. Albany: SUNY P, 2004. 35–51.

———. "Moving Writers, Shaping Motives, Motivating Critique and Change: A Genre Approach to Teaching Writing." Vandenberg, Hum, and Clary-Lemon 157–64.

Richardson, Paul W. "Language as Personal Resource and as Social Construct: Competing Views of Literacy Pedagogy in Australia." Freedman and Medway, *Learning* 117–42.

Romano, Tom. *Blending Genre, Altering Style: Writing Multigenre Papers.* Portsmouth, NH: Boynton/Cook, 2000.

———. "Teaching Writing from the Inside." *Adolescent Literacy: Turning Promise into Practice.* Ed. Kylene Beers, Robert E. Probst, and Linda Rief. Portsmouth, NH: Heinemann, 2007. 167–78.

Rubin, Susan Goldman. *The Yellow House: Vincent van Gogh and Paul Gauguin Side by Side.* Illus. Jos. A. Smith. New York: Abrams, 2001.

Russell, David. "Activity Theory and Its Implications for Writing Instruction." *Reconceiving Writing, Rethinking Writing Instruction.* Ed. Joseph Petraglia. Mahwah, NJ: Erlbaum, 1995. 51–77.

Safire, William. "How to Read a Column." *New York Times* 24 Jan. 2005. 25 Sept. 2007 <http://www.nytimes.com/2005/01/24/opinion/24safire1.html?_r=1&oref=slogin>.

Schlosser, Eric. *Fast Food Nation: The Dark Side of the All-American Meal.* New York: Perennial, 2002.

Shafer, Gregory. "Standard English and the Migrant Community." *English Journal* 90.4 (2001): 37–43.

Smagorinsky, Peter, and Michael W. Smith. "The Nature of Knowledge in Composition and Literary Understanding: The Question of Specificity." *Review of Educational Research* 62 (1992): 279–305.

Soliday, Mary. "Mapping Classroom Genres in a Science in Society Course." Herrington and Moran 65–82.

Sosnoski, James. "Hyper-readers and Their Reading Engines." *Passions, Pedagogies, and 21st Century Technologies.* Ed. Gail E. Hawisher and Cynthia L. Self. Logan: Utah State UP, 1999. 161–77.

Strong, William. *Coaching Writing: The Power of Guided Practice.* Portsmouth, NH: Heinemann, 2001.

———. *Write for Insight: Empowering Content Area Learning, Grades 6–12.* Boston: Pearson Education, 2006.

Tardy, Christine M., and John M. Swales. "Form, Text Organization, Genre, Coherence, and Cohesion." *Handbook of Research on Writing: History, Society, School, Individual, Text.* Ed. Charles Bazerman. Mahwah, NJ: Erlbaum 2007. 565–81.

Tremmel, Michelle. "Genre Theory, Narrative Theory, and Assumptions about Multigenre Writing." Diss. Michigan State U, 2003. Ann Arbor: UMI, 2003. 3100512.

Turner, Ann. *Learning to Swim: A Memoir.* New York: Scholastic, 2000.

Vandenberg, Peter, Sue Hum, and Jennifer Clary-Lemon, eds. *Relations, Locations, Positions: Composition Theory for Writing Teachers.* Urbana, IL: NCTE, 2006.

Williams, Joseph M., and Gregory G. Colomb. "The Case for Explicit Teaching: Why What You Don't Know Won't Help You." *Research in the Teaching of English* 27 (1993): 252–64.

Winchester, Simon. *The Professor and the Madman: A Tale of Murder, Insanity, and the Making of the* Oxford English Dictionary. New York: Harper, 1999.

Wirtz, Jason. "Creating Possibilities: Embedding Research into Creative Writing." *English Journal* 95.4 (2006): 23–27.

Wolff, Virginia Euwer. *Make Lemonade.* New York: Scholastic, 1993.

Wollman-Bonilla, Julie E. "Teaching Science Writing to First Graders: Genre Learning and Recontextualization." *Research in the Teaching of English* 35 (2000): 35–65.

Yancey, Kathleen Blake. *Reflection in the Writing Classroom.* Logan: Utah State UP, 1998.

Yates, JoAnne. *Control through Communication: The Rise of System in American Management.* Baltimore: Johns Hopkins UP, 1989.

Yolen, Jane, and Heidi Elisabet Yolen Stemple. *The Wolf Girls: An Unsolved Mystery from History.* Illus. Roger Roth. New York: Simon and Schuster, 2001.

Author

Photo by David Dean

Deborah Dean is associate professor of English education at Brigham Young University, where she teaches undergraduate courses in the teaching of writing and grammar, language arts teaching methods for secondary schools, and first-year and advanced writing classes. She has also taught graduate courses in composition theory and practice and has made many presentations at local and national conferences. She previously taught junior high and high school in Washington, and since moving to Utah she has volunteered as a teacher at a local high school. Dean is the author of *Strategic Writing: The Writing Process and Beyond in the Secondary English Classroom* (2006) and *Bringing Grammar to Life* (2007) and has published articles in numerous journals, including *English Journal, Voices from the Middle,* and *Journal of Adolescent and Adult Literacy*.

This book was typeset in Palatino and Helvetica by Electronic Imaging.
The typeface used on the cover was Bank Gothic.
The book was printed on 50-lb. Williamsburg Offset paper
by Midland Information Resources.